AFFILIATE MARKETING FOR BLOGGERS

All You Need To Know To Monetize Your Blog

With Affiliate Marketing From The Very Beginning

D1678365

JACOB GREEN

COPYRIGHT

Table of Contents

Introduction

Becoming a part of an affiliate network is an excellent strategy for bloggers looking to up their current income or even just to begin actually making money from their blog. There are several options when it comes to affiliate marketing as well as strategies for making affiliate marketing work for you. Below I will teach you what is affiliate marketing, examples of affiliate marketing in blogging, affiliate strategies and some of the top affiliate networks to join.

Affiliate marketing is one of the most popular ways people make money online and for some it can be a passive income once established. It is a strategy where an individual partners with a business (mainly an ecommerce site) in order to make a commission by referring readers or visitors to a business's particular product or service. But that really is quite a simple explanation. To be really successful at making money with affiliate marketing there is a little more to it.

In the case of blogging, a blogger will become an affiliate of a selected company via an affiliate network or directly from the ecommerce business, and make money from being an affiliate by placing a link, button or banner within a blog post that will lead the readers to those affiliate products or services.

A good blogger and affiliate will utilize a number of different marketing channels to promote content.

What Is Affiliate Marketing?

Affiliate marketing is an advertising model in which a company compensates third-party publishers to generate traffic or leads to the company's products and services. The third-party publishers are affiliates, and the commission fee incentivizes them to find ways to promote the company.

The Internet has increased the prominence of affiliate marketing. Amazon popularized the practice by creating an affiliate marketing program whereby websites and bloggers put links to the Amazon page for a reviewed or discussed product to receive advertising fees when a purchase is made. In this sense, affiliate marketing is essentially a pay for performance marketing program where the act of selling is outsourced across a vast network.

Affiliate marketing predates the Internet, but it is the world of digital marketing, analytics, and cookies that have made it a billion-dollar industry. A company running an affiliate marketing program can track the links that bring in leads and, through internal analytics, see how many convert to sales.

An e-commerce merchant wanting to reach a wider base of Internet users and shoppers may hire an affiliate. An affiliate could be the owner of multiple websites or email marketing lists; the more websites or email lists that an affiliate has, the wider his network. The hired affiliate then communicates and promotes the products offered on the e-commerce platform to his network. The affiliate does this by implementing banner ads, text ads, or links on its multiple owned websites or via email to its clientele. Firms use advertisements in the form of articles, videos, and images to draw an audience's attention to a service or product.

Affiliates redirect visitors who click on one of these links or ads to the e-commerce site. If they purchase the product or service, the e-commerce merchant credits the affiliate's account with the agreed-upon commission, which could be 5% to 10% of the sales price.

The goal of using an affiliate marketer is to increase sales—a win-win solution for the merchant and the affiliate.

Affiliate Marketing Examples and Strategies

What does affiliate marketing look like when you're a blogger? An example of this could be blatantly creating a post that is actually about the company you are affiliated with or you could deftly weave the product or service into a post that is on a related topic.

An example of going the blatant root? Let's say you are a food blogger and one of the companies you are an affiliate of sells food processors. You can write an entire post about that food processor including:

- ✓ Benefits

- ✓ Capabilities

- ✓ Recipes where the food processor could be utilized

- ✓ Cost

- ✓ Care instructions and more

Then you could include a button, link or banner ad that would take the reader directly to that product on an ecommerce site or platform, and they could order it based on your recommendations. Your job is to send potential customers to your affiliate program's offer.

If you would like to take a more subtle approach, include a product or service from your company that relates into your blog post. For example, let's say that you are a wine connoisseur and that is what your blog is based around. In any post that is enticing your readers to open up a good bottle of Merlot or what have you, it would be wise to embed an ad for a quality, easy-to-use wine opener, wine glasses or stoppers that keep the wine fresh.

Examples of Websites Using Affiliate Marketing

Sometimes it's a good idea to actually see some success stories within affiliate marketing to truly understand the concept of "affiliate marketing". Below I have included some real examples of websites that earn thousands of dollars per month / day, with affiliate marketing.

1. HuffingtonPost.com

Many bloggers also happen to have published more traditional collections of their writings, which allows for some affiliate marketing opportunities within any of their online pieces. Specifically, affiliate links to online retailers can be included as part of an author's articles or blog posts.

2. TopTenSelect.com

This popular product review site reviews different types of Amazon products and compiles them into comparison tables and top 10 lists. The site appears to be mainly funded by the affiliate marketing program, Amazon Associates, and only looks to gain traffic from one marketing channel (Google). The content on the site is comprehensive and gives the user great advice on what products are worth the money.

3. Dodoburd

Another insanely popular gift review site, dodoburd not only gains traffic organically from Google but they also have a strong Pinterest game. All their posts are optimized to be used on Pinterest and the content is comprehensive and well written. A great example of content marketing that fuels huge affiliate revenue growth.

Things to Avoid with Affiliate Marketing

With affiliate marketing it is best to approach content creation like you are trying to explain something to a friend or family member. Don't write like a salesperson when featuring a product or service from a company you are an affiliate of or change the tone your readers are used to.

Yes, you are in fact selling something, but your blog doesn't suddenly have to turn into a commercial or take on a voice that may be off putting to your readers. Often, bloggers will talk about how the product or service was beneficial to them while it relates to the blog's topic.

Another thing to avoid would be to display a banner or button in the post in a way that doesn't make sense or that doesn't seem to relate to the post. Give some sort of introduction to the product or a lead that particularly relates to the service so that its appearance on your blog will flow seamlessly.

Making Money As An Affiliate Marketer

How exactly does an affiliate make money? Well, believe it or not, an affiliate marketing business is probably one of the most profitable you'd likely come across. Set up correctly, it can be very lucrative. An affiliate's payment is based off of affiliate commission from the company they are an affiliate of or are paid via an affiliate marketing program or network such as Shareasale or Awin. The buttons, links or banners of the products you are trying to sell contain your unique user ID when you embed the HTML code into your blog that makes the ad appear.

When the user clicks that ad / link / image and chooses to buy the product, the company will be alerted that you were the affiliate that led them to that purchase. As such, you will receive a commission from the company for being responsible in driving traffic and new customers to their website.

How Do You Get Traffic To The Products Or Services You Are Trying To Sell?

One of the main reasons why most newbie affiliate marketers give up after 3 months is the fact that they can't build up traffic to their affiliate website. It's a thorn in most marketers' sides, but one that can be easily resolved if you put the effort in. Below I have covered a few areas that will get you good targeted traffic to your affiliate deals.

1. Create great content

Easier said than done you might say. It's true. Creating something truly amazing and resourceful takes time, effort and dedication to the project. But you don't have to reinvent the wheel. Have a look at these great content ideas that you could use for your blog.

Make your posts engaging and offer a lead that will capture readers' attention and make them want to read on and learn more about the product or service.

2. Practice effective SEO techniques

Just as with any blog post, utilising good SEO strategies and driving traffic from search engines can be a good source of quality traffic.

The skyscraping technique is a great way to not only rank for loads more keywords naturally, but also to generate links to your content by becoming the best and most comprehensive resource on the web. It's a common tactic used in online marketing for building organic traffic.

Skyscraping is when you find the best content for a particular keyword and then create your own version, but make it even better than the original. This can be done by covering areas that might be missing from your competitors piece or expanding on those topics, and become the ultimate resource for that subject.

3. Paid Traffic

The majority of affiliate marketers pay for their traffic via platforms like Facebook, Google Adwords and other ad networks. For me I'd rather gain traffic for free via search engines and social media. Be careful when promoting your affiliate links on social networks as most of them will not entertain the idea of you publishing direct links to your affiliate offers. It's always best to send social traffic to your own landing page on your site.

4. Email List

They say the money is in the list. Building up a solid email list of subscribers is one sure fire way to generate income from affiliate marketing and online marketing. Good email marketing is key. To do this you need to action some email list building ideas in order to attract people to signing up. Ideas like creating a giveaway such as a free ebook in exchange for their email works really well. Once you've built up trust with your audience, they will be more inclined to buy from your suggestions to them. This is where the money comes rolling in from affiliate sales. I can't stress enough how important it is to get onboard with email marketing, as it gives you the edge over other affiliate marketers in your niche.

5. Upsell

Upselling is a sales technique where the salesperson encourages a more expensive purchase by a customer by persuading them to get an upgraded version of an item or to purchase add-ons. Remember our food processor example? That food processor could probably be best used with a book of recipes, which also can be purchased at the same company's website. Upselling is an affiliate marketers' secret weapon to gaining extra affiliate sales.

6. Promote products you would buy

Do you have zero interest in an expensive mountain bike the company you are an affiliate of sells? Well, you probably don't want to feature it on your blog, as it is extremely difficult to persuade readers (or anyone for that matter) that they should buy something you wouldn't be caught spending a single penny on. When you are passionate about a product or–at the very least–interested in learning more about it, this will come through to your readers, engage them and better coax them to buy

Examples Of Affiliate Networks

There are several options when it comes to joining an affiliate network. It would be also be wise to join several, so that you have a variety of products and/or services at your disposal to write about and a wealth of affiliate commission.

Here are just a few that have been of great benefit to me over the years:

Amazon Associates

One of the oldest affiliate networks on the web, Amazon associates is one of the main reasons why Amazon has become the monster it is today. For me, it's been the easiest way to earn affiliate income. I have built countless Amazon niche sites where I have earned money through reviewing products that appear on Amazon.com or .co.uk

- ✓ ShareASale

- ✓ Awin

- ✓ FlexOffers

- ✓ MaxBounty

- ✓ Clickbank

If you're interested in learning more about these affiliate networks then you might want to check out my in-depth comparison of the top affiliate programs.

Advantages and Disadvantages of Affiliate Marketing

The advertising company sets the terms of an

affiliate marketing program. Early on, companies largely paid the cost per click (traffic) or cost per mile (impressions) on banner advertisements. A technology evolved, the focus turned to commissions on actual sales or qualified leads. The early affiliate marketing programs were vulnerable to fraud because clicks could be generated by software, as could impressions.

Now, most affiliate programs have strict terms and conditions on how to generate leads. There are also certain banned methods, such as installing adware or spyware that redirect all search queries for a product to an affiliate's page. Some affiliate marketing programs go as far as to lay out how a product or service is to be discussed in the content before an affiliate link can be validated.

So an effective affiliate marketing program requires some forethought. The terms and conditions must be tight, especially if the contract agreement pays for traffic rather than sales. The potential for fraud in affiliate marketing is possible.

Unscrupulous affiliates can squat on domain names with misspellings and get a commission for the redirect. They can populate online registration forms with fake or stolen information, and they can purchase AdWords on search terms the company already ranks high on, and so on. Even if the terms and conditions are clear, an affiliate marketing program requires that someone monitor affiliates and enforce rules.

Chapter One
A Focus On Affiliate Marketing

Many businesses miss out on the true benefits of affiliate marketing. As an advertiser (the business looking to obtain affiliates) you really need to understand the extremely delicate balance that needs to be achieved in order to hit that sweet spot of unbelievable business success.

So, What is This Sweet Spot Exactly?

First, this depends on the goal of your affiliate marketing campaign. For most companies there are 2 main targets that are zeroed in on:

1. Building Your Brand

2. Making a Ton of Profits

However, many businesses forget about old #3, Making a Ton of Profits for your Affiliates.

Hitting the sweet spot involves all three of these targets. I've seen a lot of companies start an affiliate program and generate a bunch of leads, and just dump their affiliates without even a care. If you do this you will miss out on a ton of money that could have been made.

You have to understand what affiliate marketing is really all about, and having been on both sides of the table (meaning I have ran affiliate programs for my business, and have also been a publisher selling affiliate products) I know exactly what needs to be achieved for both to have success.

You see, affiliate marketing is about much more than just you (the advertiser) making a great business decision to pay for only advertising that results in sales and therefore profits, it's also about building your company brand while building strategic partnerships with individuals who can literally make your business explode.

It's fine and dandy to use affiliate programs to have individuals throw up a few banner ads to make some extra money and generate leads for your business, but that's what most companies do, so why stop there? You don't want to be like everyone else, you want to be better than them. You do want to be better than them don't you? I sure hope your answer is yes, because if not you can stop reading now. You don't have to know these strategies if you don't want to, but for those who do, pay extremely close attention to the rest of this book.

Your goal with your affiliate program from this point on should be to aim for the 3 targets I mentioned earlier: Building your brand, Making a ton of profits for yourself, and Making a ton of profits for your affiliates. Helping your affiliates will help you, I can guarantee that, and this will come down to how you ultimately structure your affiliate program.

So How Do You Structure an Affiliate Program?

First, it's all about the commission. You have to give people a great incentive to advertise for you. Your goal is not just about making that quick sale (quick sales are good, but there is a lot more to this), it's about the lifetime value of the customer and building that strong brand image with them. If you don't know what the average lifetime value of your customer is, you're going to have to go through your records, do some research, and probably do a little math. At the very least you want to know how much they spend, and for how long they remain an active customer.

Typically a good commission to start with for physical products is 6-8%, and once an affiliate shows good sales volume you can increase the commission amount to 12% or even 15% if it is feasible. Keep in mind at this point, whatever commission you decide on, make sure you're still making a profit. I know that sounds like common sense to you, but later on after you've tested your campaign for a while you make actually find it more affordable to take a loss up front on the first sale. Don't worry, I'm going to cover this in a little bit, so just keep reading, but first I want to cover informational / digital product affiliate commissions.

For informational / digital download affiliate programs, you want to at least offer a 50% commission. Statistics show that programs that don't offer 50% or higher do pretty miserably. There have been a few exceptions with products I worked with that did well, but that was only because they had extremely high conversion rates. So use this as your baseline, test it, and see if you can afford to go higher. With downloadable products it's usually not the first sale that will make your business, but it's the backend products and the upsells that come later on. So just like with physical products, you want to know what the average lifetime value of a customer is, and from there, you can assess how much of a commission you can afford to give out.

Second, is cookie duration. This is very important to your affiliates because most sales do not occur on the first visit. Studies show customers on average come back between 4-7 times before a sale is actually made depending on the product that is being sold. I advise companies to use at least a 60-day cookie. Why 60? Because 30 days is the standard. Even though most sales do occur within that time period, you'll attract a ton of more affiliates with a 60-day (or greater) cookie duration.

Third, besides the cookie duration, something for you to consider is the attribution of the sale. Attribution basically means deciding on who to credit the sale to. If you have a customer who goes to one affiliate, and then doesn't buy, but a day or 2 later manages to land on a different site and then buys, who do you want to credit the sale to? Most companies prefer a last click attribute, meaning the last site to get the click that results in the sale gets the credit. This is the most common method, but there are other companies that prefer the opposite which is a first click attribute, which means even if someone bought from the second site in the above example, the site that got that first click will get the sale. Choose which rationale works for you, for me I tend to favor the last click attribute as well.

Fourth, pay your commissions on time. If you do not pay your affiliates on time they will venture somewhere else, even if it's for a lower %. Your affiliates are working hard for you and many times are paying to send traffic to their sites for the possibility of making commissions for advertising your products, and most of the time those advertising bills come in way before they get paid, and I know because I've been there. Nothing would get me more ticked off than the affiliate company not paying on time, and even worse than that, some will even wait till the next paying cycle. You need to feel your affiliates pain and know what they go through. There's nothing more agitating then spending a few hundred or thousand dollars on advertising and having to wait 2 months to get paid on it.

More Advanced Affiliate Marketing Tips For The Advertiser

So what's the point of making sure all this happens? Why is it important to make sure your affiliates are happy? Well here's some stuff that will really put you above the competition. I'm all about giving great content in my articles, so here's some juicy stuff for you.

✓ Making Outstanding Affiliate Offers

Anyone can recruit a bunch of affiliate marketers, slap up a good offer following the basics that i listed above and you'll make a bunch of sales, but will they make your business explode overnight? Probably not. It's where you take it from here that will depend on how much success your affiliate program will be. After you (or your affiliate manager) has started generating affiliates, contact them. Send a message to your affiliates and ask them if any of them would want to take advantage of a special offer, and how you'd love to work with them personally. You see many companies will give their affiliates coupon codes for shopping discounts like 5, 10, 15% off, or offer free shipping for people that buy through affiliate links. Now these work pretty decent from time to time, they do help people to buy through affiliates, but there is always a way to take things one step above the competition, and that's what I'm going to teach you here.

✓ Typical Multi-Product Website Affiliate Offers

You want to work closely with a few select individuals that responded to that email that you sent to them about working with them personally. Depending on your business structure, there are a few directions you can go from here. First I want to talk about your standard multi-product website. Let's say you sell furniture online and really want to get your business to explode. Instead of just giving coupons to your affiliates you want to try to get your affiliates to promote different categories or even a specific product in ways that aren't possible through your site.

Let me explain, a typical product website can only do so much. You have a product picture, a description, maybe a bit of ad copy, and a price. The only factors that you can really change to increase sales are Price, Free or Reduced Shipping, tweak the Copy, and Brand Image. This is pretty standard stuff, and there's nothing wrong with it, but there is a whole other level that you can hit with your affiliates, but will not be able to fly on your site. Since we're talking about furniture, let's say you have a product that you want to work with an affiliate to sell. The product is called the Super Deluxe Bed. With your chosen affiliate there are a lot more things you can work on to get this product sold. An affiliate (with your supervision) can create copy for the product that will be able to incorporate so many other sales triggers to get it sold.

Example: Your affiliate is promoting the Super Deluxe Bed. For his customers you allow him to have an exclusive offer (or allow him to say it's exclusive) for this bed, and that the only way they'll get this exclusive offer is if their customers buy through him. However, that's just the beginning. Allow your affiliate to inject some scarcity into his customers veins. Make it an "Extremely Limited" offer that's only available for a limited time, or that you're only allowing a certain # of these beds to be sold at this price. You can also allow your affiliate to offer a bonus to the customers that buy the Super Deluxe Bed. The bonus can either be a physical product like a "limited edition lamp", or a Free "How to Get an Amazing Nights Sleep" Special Report. Salesmanship like this will get a ton of more products sold for you.

Exploding Your Business With Affiliate Marketing

These are things that will get your business to literally explode but something you can't do alone. If you did this on your site for every product or category you would come off as too salesy, or too pushy. I mean think about it, if every product bought got the same special bonus it wouldn't be special any more, or if everything is listed as "limited quantities available" you'd seem more like a business that can't manage it's stock rather than one that's giving people an "exclusive limited offer".

Really take a few minutes to picture the 2 different sales processes I just described, and put yourself in the customers shoes to feel the experience they would have in each situation. Which do you think would be more likely to make the sale: Your site listing the product with free shipping, or an affiliate site listing the product with an "exclusive limited time free shipping offer", with a bonus (only for the next 10 orders) Free "How to Get an Amazing Nights Sleep" Special Report (a $37 value), along with some longer more compelling copy?

See you can't do that with every product on your own site, but with the power of affiliate marketing you can drive highly targeted traffic to amazing offers like this without tarnishing your brand. It's really just unbelievable how doing this with multiple affiliates with several different products or categories can blow away the competition and make you and your affiliates a lot of money, and I'm just talking about visitors coming to your site via advertising, don't even let me get started with what this process can do for you in a product or business launch or relaunch sequence. Ever want to know what it's like to make a year's worth of sales in a few days? You just try this in a launch or relaunch and the results will surely make your eyes plunge out of their sockets.

✓ Information Product Website Affiliate Offers

For an Information / Digital Download type of site, you can use the same techniques as above. Work with your affiliates to allow them to offer something unique specifically for their customers. Either you can create it for them or let them do it with your supervision of course. The point is to make it so that your affiliate is giving them something exclusive for ordering through them. Also, just like with the physical products above, If you do a well coordinated product launch with your affiliates you can expect to make a lot of cash quickly.

Why You Need to Keep Your Affiliates For the Long Term

So why do you want your affiliates to succeed so badly? What do you need them for after the sale is made? I mean you got your money your leads, what else can they possibly be good for? Because your affiliates, if you work with them and help train them with the example techniques I mentioned in this report, they will always continue to bring you high quality leads. You always want to allow them to make available to their customers "highly exclusive" offers on a continuous basis. Don't forget, affiliates one way or another through using their time or cold hard cash, that they are covering your advertising expenses.

✓ Making a Profit Selling at a Loss

Remember way up at the top of this article when I mentioned sometimes you can have an affiliate program where you can actually take a loss up front on the first sale? Well, I want to get into that here a bit like I promised. You see, making that first sale is what is crucial to your affiliate marketers, it's what gets their motor going. If you can afford to take a loss up front then do it and you'll see more affiliates then you can handle sign up for your program, but only if you have an awesome backend to sell those customers, and this is something that requires testing. If you're not making a profit, don't do it. Your backend, whether digital download or physical product, has to make you a nice profit. I'm not talking nickles and dimes, I mean a hefty profit. I know the bulk of this article talks about being good to your affiliates, but you're in this to make money and they understand that. They may be taking on the bulk of your advertising expenses, but you're here to make a profit too. If you're going to go for a loss on the front end, you don't give your affiliates backend commissions unless you're making huge profits yourself, but if you structure it so that you can make some good money on the front end, there's no problem with thanking your affiliates with a nice commission on that as well.

✓ Building Your Brand With Affiliate Marketing

Throughout this whole affiliate program process remember your targets. You now know how to make a ton of money for yourself and your affiliates, but don't you dare forget about that brand! You must build your company's brand in with the affiliate marketing process. Even though the link of the product will be redirecting to your site, your site's name needs to be on that page. Those customers need to know that those Super Deluxe Bed "exclusive offers" are going to Squiggly Doo's Furniture Store before the link sends them there. It really helps the credibility of the switch from one site to the next. Take note however, that you are not endorsing any bonuses (anything separate from your sites offers) that may be offered through your affiliates, you're just privately approving them. It's just a matter of protecting your brand, and guarding yourself legally. If you find yourself getting complaints about the bonuses being offered, look into the matter immediately and notify the affiliate to stop offering it because your brand is your #1 long term asset.

Your brand is what will keep those customers coming back to you for repeat business and continually buying your products. Another reason why you want to keep your affiliates for the long term is because if they know the right techniques (which you'll enlighten them with) they will build deep relationships with the people that just bought through their link. So you want to encourage your affiliates to build a list and stay in close contact with your shared customers so they can continually promote for you, and both make a lot of money. So for your benefit, reach out to your affiliates and make sure they can capture leads effectively. It's much easier to have individual affiliates build those relationships with you're customers as opposed to having it all on you. With you and your affiliate marketers working as a team you all will make lots of cash, and build a solid brand.

Is Affiliate Marketing the Right Move For You?

Thousands, if not millions, of online webmasters and marketers are turning to affiliate marketing to earn extra money from the web. Affiliate marketing offers the perfect way for the ordinary person to cash in on the billions of sales made online each year.

<u>But is Affiliate Marketing right for you?</u>

Is it something that you should investigate and pursue further if you truly want to monetize your site or content? As a way of an answer and to get you thinking about affiliate marketing; I would like to offer some of my own experiences as a full-time online affiliate marketer. I would also like to give you some marketing tips and a few pit-falls you should try to avoid.

Truth be told, I didn't plan to become an affiliate marketer. It just happened, mostly by accident, as I was struggling to promote my first site on Internet marketing some 10 years ago now. My original plan was to re-sell some software products with hopes of making my fortune on this new thing called the Internet.

Well, to make a long story short, most things don't quite turn out as we originally plan. Instead of selling my own products, I became much more interested in studying "how to market online" and examining "how marketing systems worked" than actually selling my own stuff. I was much more fascinated in the "nuts & bolts" or "marketing tools" behind these online marketing systems than earning a few pennies.

I was particularly captivated by a new search engine called Google. Yes, there are many marketers around who have been studying Google since it first started. And I believe it was Google and its AdSense Program in particular that sort of legitimized the "whole idea of making money online" for me. I turned my attention to other ways of monetizing my sites, especially with affiliate programs. And the rest as they say is history.

But enough about me, what about you?

Do you have a website? Are you interested in earning extra revenue from your site? Are you trying to earn a full-time income online? More importantly:

Is Affiliate Marketing Right for you?

First, you have to realize Affiliate Marketing is when you promote and sell affiliate products from your site or sites. Actually, selling is not quite the right word because you DON'T actually sell anything from your site. You merely refer or send customers/interested buyers to the affiliate sites you're promoting via your affiliate links.

Believe me, sometimes this concept is very hard to explain to close family and friends. But what do you sell online? You don't have anything to sell? How can you make money?

To repeat, with affiliate marketing you don't sell anything directly online... you send clients and customers to online companies or merchants where they buy stuff and since they're coming from your site's affiliate links you get credit for the sale.

I don't directly sell Dell Computers on my sites, I merely send prospective customers to Dell where they can buy Dell products and since they came from my affiliate links I get credit, plus a small commission in return if they buy something. Same goes for Amazon or hundreds of the other companies and products I promote with my sites.

Now Affiliate Marketing Fits Me to a Tee! Here's why...

✓ You don't handle any sales transactions

✓ You don't handle any delivery of products

✓ You don't have to deal with customer complaints or run customer support

✓ You don't have to manage employees or operate a business

✓ You don't need an office, stock, or any physical products

With Affiliate Marketing all the selling and business operations are done by the company you're promoting. This saves you from a lot of headaches and problems that arise from running your own company or developing your own products. It's all done for you.

Furthermore, online Affiliate Marketing does have some great advantages:

✓ Your sites and affiliate links are working for you 24/7, 365 days of the year. You earn sales/commissions while you're sleeping, eating, watching TV or doing anything we humans do!

✓ You earn money even when you're on Vacation. This happened to me last year when I went to Florida to see Bruce Springsteen in concert. Unfortunately, a band member died so I didn't get to see Springsteen but I did make more than enough online to pay for my whole trip WHILE I was in Orlando. It was also the first time, I didn't have access to my computer or sites for more than a few days, but they still made me money.

Once you get your affiliate links set-up, they will continue to earn you revenue automatically. All your online marketing can be automated and run from your home office or from anywhere you choose.

Keep in mind, your content and sites keep building and growing. Work you did writing that great article two years ago is still bringing in affiliate sales today. Plus, with Affiliate Marketing, all your marketing materials (banners, sales copy, videos, ads, links...) are all provided for you by the Affiliate Network or

Company.

There's little stress with affiliate marketing mainly because you're your own boss and you can work at home. No office politics or all that foolishness. No commuting. In addition, there is very little capital investment, for a few hundred dollars or much less, you can have a site up and running on the web.

However, Affiliate Marketing does have some real disadvantages:

✓ You can often earn much more if you develop and sell your own products. You're not really getting the highest return on your site's content by selling other people's stuff. The profit margin can be much, much higher if you sell your own products.

✓ There is also the issue of lost commissions and theft of sales, you can never be sure you're getting credit for all your traffic and referrals. In most cases you're not.

✓ Many times there's stiff competition from other affiliates selling the same stuff and using the same marketing materials... although many top affiliates create their own marketing materials so they stand out in a crowded marketplace.

Since I am a full-time online affiliate marketer blogger the benefits far outweigh the few downers associated with this great lifestyle. Mainly because it is just that: a lifestyle rather than a job. I never think of it as a job or working. Maybe, that's because I am my own master, I can work from home and set my own hours. I can take time off, I can go on vacations or I can live anywhere in the world where there's Internet Access and these days that's just about anywhere. The sense of freedom is truly intoxicating to say the least.

If you do find Affiliate Marketing is something that you would like to pursue, even part-time if not full-time, here are some of my best tips for increasing your affiliate income and sales:

Focus your marketing efforts and attention on programs and products which give you recurring or residual income. Make one sale and get paid for years to come.

Develop your own sites and marketing materials so that you stand out from the other affiliate marketers. Create your own unique selling position even if you're not technically selling the products. Give extra bonuses if they buy from your links or site.

✓ Build your own list of customers who are

interested in the products you're promoting. Grow your own list, as well as that of the affiliate company you're promoting. You will always have these subscribers and you can promote other similar products to them.

✓ Concentrate on targeting "long tail keywords" with your content and sites; these multi-worded keyword phrases are easy to rank high for and usually have better conversion rates.

✓ Cloak your affiliate links to cut down on affiliate theft. For example, ClickBank has a simple HTML code that will hide your link. Use it.

Internet users and especially shoppers want simple helpful information to make their buying decisions easier. Provide them with valuable information they can use in their task and they will reward you with a sale. Also giving away coupons and online discounts will increase your sales and commissions.

✓ Use the major affiliate networks like Commission Junction, LinkShare, ClickBank, Amazon, Shareasale... I have found these networks very simple to use and very effective. Plus, their checks never bounce!

✓ Keep a close eye on your monthly sales, with many of the companies if you go over $25,000 or $50,000 in sales for the month, you get extra bonus incentives. I have found these can dramatically increase your monthly income so watch your sales stats closely.

If you do find that Affiliate Marketing is right for you, chances are almost 100% certain that you will never regret it. Affiliate marketing offers one of the least stressful ways of earning a living on the planet and the lifestyle can't be beat. Anyone can change their lives with affiliate marketing. I did and you can too!

Chapter Two
Affiliate Marketing Vs Product Creation

This is a huge obstacle many people face when entering the online marketing world: Should I become an affiliate marketer or should I create and sell my own product..?

Before I get started let me quickly define the two business models so that we are clear as to how money is generated with each.

✓ Affiliate Marketing:

In this business model you will be making income by referring customers to another person's product or service. So basically you will sign up with the vendor as an affiliate and for every sale you generate you get paid a commission.

✓ Product Creation:

This business model is pretty self explanatory; you will be creating a product and selling it in the marketplace for 100% of the profits. In this example we will be assuming your product is an information product of some sort.

There are a lot of marketers that will say the easiest way to start making money online is affiliate marketing. Just because of the simple fact that you can choose a vendor whose product you want to promote, sign up as an affiliate, start sending traffic to your affiliate sales page and BOOM! You make money. Sounds pretty easy. You don't have to deal with creating a product, setting up websites, dealing with customers, etc.

At the same time there are marketers that say creating your own product is easier and the more profitable of the two and allows you to be more in control of your business. It really all depends on what your strengths and weaknesses are and what you're looking to accomplish in your business.

Let me get some of the pros and cons of each and put things into perspective so you can have a better idea of where you want to get started.

It is a strong argument that affiliate marketing is the easier of the two to start with which is why it is recommended as a starting point for beginners.

Here are a few of the pros of affiliate marketing:

✓ Most affiliate vendors/networks are free and

very easy to join. Most of the time you will answer a few basic questions, set up a username and password and get instant access to the affiliate member's area within a few minutes.

✓ Marketing materials are provided. Once you set up your profile in the affiliate member's area you will have complete access to all marketing materials needed to get you going such as banners, pre-written emails, etc. In the members area you will also be provided a unique affiliate link which will take your prospects to a complete sales page which has already been created for you. Armed with these materials all you have to focus on is getting traffic to your affiliate site.

✓ All websites are already created for you. As an affiliate you do not have to deal with the headaches that can come with setting up a website. The vendor has done this for you and as long as you use your affiliate link your sales and commissions will be tracked through that link and paid into your account.

✓ Do not have to deal with customers. We all know how difficult it can be to deal with customers but as an affiliate you do not have to worry about this problem. Once you make a sale as an affiliate all you have to worry about is cashing your check and the customer is passed on to the vendor.

As you can see being an affiliate marketer definitely has its perks. It's quick and easy to join a vendor/network, all the marketing materials and sales pages are provided and you do not have to deal with customers. You can focus your time on generating traffic, making sales and cashing checks!

Now let's take a look at some of the cons of affiliate marketing and how you can overcome them.

- ✓ The competition. Even though it can argued that affiliate marketing is the easiest way to make money online it can be strongly argued that it's the most difficult due to the competition. There are hundreds of thousands of affiliate marketers you have to compete with to make a sale. At the same time many experienced marketers agree that most new affiliate marketers do not know what they're doing since it's such an easy business to get into.

One of the best ways to overcome this obstacle is to educate yourself. Always be a step ahead of the competition by learning what the top affiliates are doing to give them that edge needed to make the sale.

- ✓ Profit Margins. As I mentioned before with affiliate marketing you are making a commission for referring a customer to a vendor as opposed to you being the creator of the product and earning 100% of the sale. So there can be a lot of profits you are leaving on the table by promoting someone else's product instead of your own.

This obstacle is really not in your control when it comes to affiliate marketing but the best thing you can do is promote a product with a higher payout of 60-80% as opposed to 25-50%. This way you will be making more income with less sales.

- ✓ Building someone else's business. As an affiliate not only are you generating sales and profits for the vendor you are also helping them build their business instead of your own. Once you make a sale and are paid a commission that customer is now in the hands of the vendor which can continue to sell additional products and services to that customer for the lifetime of their relationship.

The best way I know of building your own business through affiliate marketing while also sending customers to the vendor is to set up a landing page of your own that requires the prospect to input their name and email before they get access to the sales page. This way the prospect is on your customer list as well and you can now email them future offers and affiliate products directly. Now of course you will have to provide an incentive to the prospect for them to enter their email like giving away a free report, video training, audio file, etc. We will touch on this in a future report.

✓ Lack of control. With affiliate marketing you really don't have much control of anything but generating sales. Should the vendor/network decide to shut down or no longer sell the product you are promoting you are left back at square one. When it comes to product creation you have a lot more control of your business but we'll be touching on that in a few.

Unfortunately this is a huge downside to affiliate marketing and something you really can't prepare for. Building your email list as mentioned before is the best way to ensure that you still have an ability to make sales with your current list of customers while you set up a new campaign with a new product.

There are just as many cons as pros with affiliate

marketing but none of these reasons should stop you from getting started if it's a business you wish to pursue. One important thing that you want to keep in mind is to take time to invest in your education and skill sets to put yourself ahead of the curve. By doing this you set yourself apart from the competition and a step ahead to making the sale.

If you are interested in learning more about affiliate marketing and jump starting your way to success visit my author resource box.

Now, just for a second picture yourself being the product creator and having an army of affiliates promoting your products as we move into the pros and cons of Creating and selling your own product.

1. Product Creation

Product creation can be a scary subject for many because as a newbie you are most likely skeptical and completely in the dark as to how an online business operates, let alone creating a product from scratch. But to your surprise it can actually be one of the easiest ways to make money online.

Let's get into some of the pros of creating and selling your own product and see why it can be an avenue you consider:

✓ Control.

When it comes to product creation you are in complete control of just about everything. You are in control of how you market your product, the price, its delivery, and you are in full control of every customer you bring into your business as well as any future purchases they make from you.

✓ Profits.

Of course this is a huge reason why many people create and sell their own products. As a product creator you get to keep 100% of the profits from every sale you make. Now there is an exception to this when it comes to setting up your own affiliate program and having other affiliates promote your products but we'll touch on the power of this next.

✓ Affiliates.

Once you create your unique product you can choose to leverage others to help build your business. Setting up an affiliate program can be a powerful way to explode your business on autopilot. You can offer your affiliates a commission of 30-50% and have them sell their butts off for you especially if your product brings high value to the marketplace. Also you can make money while you sleep as you know your affiliates are working hard to make you sales.

✓ Building a Brand.

Being the product creator gives you the opportunity to build a brand for yourself in the marketplace of your chosen topic. Since your product is unique you are able to name the product whatever you like and build a brand around that topic. This is very big if you want to build your business through word-of-mouth advertising which we all know is the strongest form of advertising.

As you can see there are also some great advantages to creating and selling your own product. You are in full control of everything, you will earn more money, you can build an army of affiliates, and you can build a brand for yourself and your business. But as in everything there is a downside so let's get into that next.

Here are a few cons of product creation and how you can overcome them:

✓ Time.

When it comes to your time, creating your own product will definitely take up more of your time than simply signing up as an affiliate. Not only will it take time to create your product, but you also have to create a website to sell your product from. And that can be a headache of its own which we will talk about next.

The great thing about product creation is you can outsource just about every process involved in starting your business. You can literally pay a professional writer to write your information product for you and you take the credit for it. Of course you always want to proof read it and modify a bit to fit your personality and style.

✓ Websites.

Once your product is completed you will not be able to make any profit unless you are able to get it published online. For some this can be your worst nightmare. This can cause you a lot of headaches especially if you are not tech savvy. This can easily cause you to quit or never begin to try to make money online, or it can cause you to have to hire a web designer to build a site for you which can be a few hundred to a few thousand dollars in cost. This leads me to my next topic.

Again building a website can easily be outsourced to a web designer who can build you a clean professional website usually within 48-72 hours.

✓ Cost.

When it comes to creating a product it can easily be said you will have more start up costs then an affiliate. When it comes to setting up your sales funnel you have certain costs like buying a domain, hosting your website, hiring a web designer to set up you site unless you're doing it yourself, paying for the graphics to brand your product, etc.

A lot of you may be asking yourself how much are you going to expect to spend on your product creation business? Don't worry take a deep breath..a lot of the things you will be paying for are really inexpensive. You can buy a domain for about $10 and hosting is about $5 a month. Now I want to introduce you to a site that will dramatically change the way you do business it's called http://www.Fiverr.com. This is a community of people that are willing to just about anything for $5. Go ahead and visit the site and see for yourself. You can literally have an information product created on a topic of your choice, the graphics and ebook cover created, and a website build for $25-$30.

✓ Customer Support.

As the product owner you will be responsible for your customer service and support and this alone can drive you insane and drain a lot of your time and energy. As in any business on or offline you will have your happy customers and your not so happy customers. Your customers will have questions, demands, concerns, etc and it is your responsibility to make sure they get the support they deserve.

Jacob Green

Customer support can also be outsourced but unfortunately this comes with the territory of any business and something you will have to deal with. Yes you can have someone take care of your customers service but you should definitely be as involved as possible to make sure they are getting the best support possible.

As you can see as a product owner, yes you will be in control, yes you will make more money, and yes you can build a brand, but with all this comes a lot more responsibility then an affiliate marketer.

Before wrapping things up lets touch on a few things that we can all agree on in both affiliate marketing and product creation.

2. Work from home.

Whether you are an affiliate marketer or promoting your own products both allow you to be in control of your time and work from home. For many this a highly sought after luxury to be able to spend more time with family, friends, spouse, etc.

3. Your day job.

Unless you are a super marketer and were born with super online business skills most of you will still be working your day job as you build your online business. With that said you can build your online business on a part-time or full-time basis around your current work schedule whether it is one hour a day or ten hours a day whatever it is that works for you make sure you keep it consistent. Make sure you schedule your online business time just as you would schedule any other activity and make this non-negotiable.

4. You're the boss.

No matter if you're marketing as an affiliate or your own product, you are your own boss in both situations and your income is directly influenced by your efforts. This also allows you to make money on demand. If you're looking to take a vacation or buy a new car and you need a few thousand dollars you can just jump on your computer and set up a new marketing campaign.

In sumary there is really no right or wrong, better or worse, that was not the point of this article. The point of this report was to shed some light on both business models so that you can be more aware of what you can expect in moving forward with your online business. In my opinion there shouldn't have to be a choice between affiliate marketing and creating your own product. You should integrate both into your business plan and become educated in both arenas. By doing that you will quickly see that many top affiliate marketers make a killing selling their own products and many people who sell their own products make a killing as affiliate marketers.

One thing I do want to stress is no matter what you do it is going to take time, effort and hard work. Don't fall into the trap that many newbie's do which is consistently searching for the next plug and play system that is going to make you the next overnight millionaire. And there are plenty of "Guru's" out there who prey on the newbie community and put out junk products promising overnight millions with pretty sales pages and you continue to fall for them. STOP!! Map out a business plan, decide what you want to accomplish, find one reputable mentor you want to follow and get to work! Focus on following that chosen mentor all the way through to your first online dollar. Lastly, make a promise to yourself that you will not quit before starting the journey!

The Power and Profits of Affiliate Marketing

Affiliate marketing is one of the most effective and powerful ways of earning money online. This is an opportunity that gives everybody a chance to make a profit through the Internet.

Affiliate marketing is flourishing and spreading

across the internet at an incredibale rate. Some would argue that the future for Affiliate Marketing is as far reaching as that of the internet itself. Affiliate Marketing is an agreement between a merchant and a website owner. The website owner, or the affiliate, allows the use of their site for the promotion of the merchant's products by linking to the merchant's website.

Affiliate Marketing is selling on behalf of someone else in return for a percentage of the sale. You stock no product, don't need to package or handle, nor do you have the normal business overheads.

Affiliate marketing is often called, "performance-based-marketing", meaning you don't pay the advertiser until they sell something. Affiliate marketing ensures that you only pay when your ad results in a sale.

Affiliate marketing is nothing more than commissioned sales on the Internet. The affiliate is a commissioned salesperson for a specific product or service which he is promoting through online advertising.

Affiliate marketing is a really easy way to get started online. The reason for this is that it is a lot of work to create a product and learn all the skills required to make money online. Affiliate marketing is one of the biggest markets on the internet today.

More so than any other type of business, people are hanging up their traditional nine to five jobs and joining the internet bandwagon. Affiliate Marketing is the fine art of selling other people's stuff online, usually through your own website.

I believe that Affiliate Marketing is the fastest, easiest, and most effective way to break into the Internet Marketing field of business and I also believe it is one of the best Home Businesses you can start.

Affiliate Marketing is simply the art of selling products for a company. It's like being a Car Salesman who works on commission, except as a car salesman you can't sell just any car (in most cases). Affiliate Marketing is a way for advertisers to reach potential customers and only pay when a visitor takes some predefined action. Predefined actions range from a sale to registration.

Affiliate marketing is a gamble. That's no secret to affiliates rolling the dice every day on new offers and campaigns.

Affiliate marketing isn't for the weak of heart. If you want to be successful and make money from it, you need determination and motivation. Affiliate marketing is tough. Anyone who tells you different is most likely very very smart, or very very stupid.

Affiliate marketing is really about working with partners to help market or even sell your products. Think of how authors often put the Amazon widget on their blog to sell their book in hopes they get a small residual.

Affiliate marketing is both an effective and powerful way to earn money online. The affiliate marketing programs are easy to join and implement. Affiliate Marketing is the most promising and lucrative business model on the internet.

There are millions of affiliate marketers but there is more than adequate money for everyone out there. Affiliate Marketing is the relationship between website owners and merchants whereby the merchant offers the website owner (affiliate) commission for linking to his/her merchant site.

Affiliates send traffic to the merchant site through these affiliate links and the affiliate is rewarded each time a visitor converts to a sale (CPA) or lead (CPL). Affiliate Marketing is definitely a system that works. Affiliate marketing is the Home Business model that CAN bring you home business success, without outlaying a cent.

Do yourself a favor DO IT NOW! Affiliate marketing is not easy work but it's definitely a good way to build a side business that could have the potential to be a full time job.

10 Affiliate Marketing Management Tips For Bloggers

Discover The Answer To The 10 Most Common Affiliate Marketing Management Questions

1. Is affiliate marketing right for my business?

Affiliate marketing is one of the most powerful and effective means of gaining new customers, regardless of your product or service. Affiliate marketing exposes your business to new customers and can get you out of your marketing rut. Additionally, when you initiate an affiliate marketing campaign, you're in control. You determine the commission rate you pay and pay only when your affiliates make a sale. It's a no loss operation for you because you only pay when a sale is made.

2. What are the startup costs?

When you start an affiliate program you have the choice of handling the operations yourself or having it managed by an affiliate network. The costs for either choice are reasonable and generally start around a few hundred dollars. Additionally, as a business owner don't forget that many of your costs may be tax deductible. To start an affiliate marketing program in house, costs will include:

Affiliate management software

Affiliate marketing support including a website that answers affiliate questions and a means for them to contact you if any issues arise. Affiliate marketing materials including banner ads, copy, coupons, and promotional content.

If you choose to hire an affiliate network to handle your program, they generally charge a flat fee or a percentage of what you pay out each month.

3. How much time will it take out of my workday/workweek?

Most experts agree that it will take you about an hour and a half each day to manage your affiliate program. They also recommend you to budget more time in the first few months of your program, approximately two to three hours a day. Even the most efficient affiliate managers spend about 45 minutes a day managing their affiliate program.

Professional affiliate managers generally spend an average of 40-80 hours a month dedicated to managing, tracking and promoting your affiliate program.

4. Should I use an affiliate network?

Do you have an extra 3 hours a day for the next two or three months? Do you have an hour a day to devote to managing your program after the initial three month program is complete? An affiliate network, while it may be a bit more expensive on the outset, can help you focus your time on other profit generating tasks. Additionally, an affiliate network can help expose your affiliate program to a wide variety of experience affiliates, which means more money in your bottom line and more exposure overall.

That being said, there are a tremendous number of effective in-house solutions including some you're likely already familiar with like 1shoppingcart.com and affiliatepro.com. These programs will help you stay 100% in control of your affiliate program and are effective at managing your program.

5. How should I pay affiliates? What type of commission works best?

This is a very important decision because it not only affects your profits, the right commission rate will help you recruit top-notch affiliates. The general rule of thumb is to set your default commission rate at a rate you can afford to pay while leaving room for time limited commission increase offers, promotions, and private offers. For example, if you can afford to pay 50% of your gross profit margin, pay 25% instead and tier it so that after a sales goal is reached they earn 30% or you can bump it up to 50% during the holidays or during typically low sales times.

6. How do I recruit affiliates?

Your customers may be your best affiliates. After all, they already appreciate and enjoy your products or services. A simple link on your website is a good place to start. Here are a few ways to find quality affiliates:

Online forums. These are excellent places to meet and greet and connect with like minded individuals. They're also a good resource for affiliates who are interested in, motivated, and qualified to sell your products and services. Using a forum, you can announce your affiliate program. Be careful to not 'sell' on the forum as most forums look down on this and may kick you off. Additionally, you can include a link to your affiliate site in your signature.

Find websites that link to your competitors and approach them about being an affiliate for you. Likewise, you can find affiliates using your favorite search engine and contact them about joining your program.

One last way is to join an affiliate network or become listed on an affiliate directory. This will allow you to find affiliate marketers who are searching for new products and services to promote. However, keep in mind that many beginner marketers also seek products and services to promote via affiliate directories and they may lose interest and motivation before they ever make a sale. This isn't a strong deterrent because they don't get paid unless they make a sale, however it should be noted.

7. What is the best way to communicate with my affiliates?

Email is the general tool of choice, which makes an auto responder a fantastic tool for basic emails like the welcome email, introducing promotions, coupons, sending links and banner ads, and answering Frequently Asked Questions. It is also generally advisable to have an email address, fax number, and telephone number available for when affiliates have questions that are not answered by your frequently asked questions web page or when they simply want to speak with you.

8. How do I motivate affiliates?

Money motivates no doubt about it. That being

said, affiliates are also motivated by feeling that they're important to you. This means when they ask for your time, you give it. Additionally, promotions, bonuses, prizes, contests, and commission increases are all tools to motivate and inspire affiliates. Constant communication, like sending a weekly or monthly Ezine, will also help remind your affiliates that you're out there and invested in their success.

9. Do I need to hire an affiliate manager?

The answer to this question really depends on your needs. How large is your company? Do you have the time to manage your program? Do you have the skills to manage your program? An affiliate manager is the person that:

- ✓ Recruits affiliates

- ✓ Communicates with affiliates

- ✓ Develops, tracks, and reports on promotions

- ✓ Develops programs to enhance the affiliate program

- ✓ Motivates affiliates

- ✓ Tracks sales and pays affiliates

- ✓ Monitors your competition

These are all extremely important functions and if you have the time to handle them yourself, excellent! If you do not, then consider hiring an affiliate manager.

10. How do I find/hire an affiliate manager?

Outsourcing an affiliate manager is fairly easy to do. There are hundreds available with a quick online search. You can ask associates, inquire at online forums, or post an advertisement seeking someone to fill the position. Depending on the complexity of your affiliate program, you could consider a well qualified virtual assistant for the job. The skills your affiliate manager will need are:

- ✓ Organizational skills

- ✓ Communication skills

- ✓ Attention to detail

- ✓ Knowledge of online business, internet marketing, and basic ecommerce operations

- ✓ Basic html and graphic experience are a plus

Because they're going to be representing you, you'll want to make sure they're personable.

Chapter Three
Best Affiliate Programs For Bloggers

Over the past six years, I've gone from learning how to start a blog, to now reaching more than 500,000+ monthly readers and earning upwards of $50,000/mo—mostly from the blogger affiliate programs I'm a member of.

Along the way, I've learned which affiliate programs are genuinely beneficial to both bloggers and readers, which programs convert really well and even how to find new affiliate programs that have the most appealing offers for your readers.

Now, if you're like any of the bloggers I know... the purpose of joining an affiliate program is to get financially compensating for the content you already want to write on your blog anyway. Affiliate programs are one of the best (and easiest) ways to start making money from your blog regardless of how many readers you have today.

For those of you that may think it's too competitive to launch a blog today, here's a powerful statistic...

it's widely reported that affiliate marketing is set to reach \$6.8 billion by 2020. So, even if you're brand new to blogging, carving out your niche in the market—and joining the right affiliate programs can still be incredibly lucrative.

Choosing which affiliate programs are best as a blogger can be tricky, however. Especially if you're doing this for the first time. With literally thousands of affiliate programs available—and more being added to emerging verticals every day—it can get difficult to hone in on the best options for you.

In this roundup, I'm shining a light on a small sampling of what's out there... only the best of the best affiliate programs for bloggers to join right away.

What is an Affiliate Program? (For Bloggers)

An affiliate program is an arrangement by which a company (online merchant) selling a product, tool or service—agrees to pay their affiliates (you) a commission for any sales your blog generates of their products or services.

For the company who manages the affiliate program, they're incentivizing you (with commission payouts) to send them referral traffic. It's one of the easiest ways for brands to attract new customers, because they're tapping into blogs (like yours) where their target audience already exists online. The process works by placing an affiliate link on your blog, which leads anyone who clicks on it straight to the merchant's website.

The agreements of affiliate programs often vary greatly—some offer a commission to the affiliate only after a customer completes a sale, while other affiliate programs offer a commission for just getting a visitor to sign up for a free trial of their product—whether or not they end up becoming a fully paid customer.

There's also a vast difference when it comes to commission rates too, which is why you need to do your homework and consider many factors before you make the choice to go with a particular affiliate program. That's a major reason why I compiled this list of the best affiliate programs for bloggers to get started with today.

In short though, there are three main types of rewards in affiliate marketing:

1. **Free Product:** With product-based affiliate marketing, when you promote a brand's products, you'll get free samples,

credits or plan upgrades in exchange for referring new customers to the company. While this can sometimes be a win, it's not the best way to make money blogging, so we don't have any of those programs included on this list.

2. **Commission:** Most affiliate programs will compensate you for each time a new customer signs up for a company's product, tool or service via your affiliate link, granting you a one-time fixed commission payout (sometimes based on the value of which plan or product the customer purchased).

3. **Percentage of Sale:** This is by far, the most common type of affiliate marketing, mainly because it's considered to be more worthwhile. Under this agreement, you will receive a percentage of the sales whenever someone clicks on the affiliate link on your blog/website and purchases the product or service being offered on the other side.

How Do You Join an Affiliate Program?

When it comes to joining an affiliate program, bloggers often have two choices: self-hosted programs and those programs that are available on major affiliate networks.

A self-hosted affiliate program runs on the company's own website, using either internally built or white-labeled affiliate software. All you have to do is a quick Google search of "brand + affiliate program" and you'll find a link to more information about their affiliate program:

Alternatively, many brands choose to host their affiliate programs inside of larger affiliate networks, like ShareASale or ClickBank. These massive affiliate network platforms allow you to find and join multitudes of new affiliate programs in different verticals, view commission rates and track reports all under one roof.

That being said, these networks can sometimes be restricted a bit in terms of options and commission payouts, which is why you should always first check if a company hosts their affiliate program through their own website first (where commission rates will be highest). Regardless of which route you take, some programs will add you automatically once you've reached certain benchmarks, while others accept anyone who applies to promote their products.

All bloggers need in order to join an affiliate program, is a website—which I'm guessing you already have if you're a blogger—and a way to receive payments. The most common way to be paid out by an affiliate program is through PayPal, via direct deposit or even by Venmo.

I'd also recommend getting yourself a dedicated email address that'll be connected to your domain, which will make you more legitimate in the eyes of the companies you'll (soon) be applying to promote. Make sure your blog also has an SSL certificate, so that all connections to your website will be secure (HTTPS) for your readers—because most companies want to know their affiliates take their blog security seriously.

Now that we've got the introductory affiliate marketing stuff out of the way, it's time to dive into the best affiliate programs for bloggers to leverage.

1. Amazon Associates

Who hasn't heard of Amazon? This platform is a giant in the eCommerce world and its popularity continues to grow. So, if you ever talk about products that could potentially be for sale somewhere on Amazon, then it makes sense for you to join Amazon Associates to begin collecting (small) commissions on the products people purchase after following your Amazon affiliate links.

Here's a quick breakdown of the commission rates Amazon currently offers on their main product categories:

- ✓ **Commission Rate**: Varies between 1.0% and 10.0% depending on the product category.

- ✓ **Payment Method:** Direct bank deposit, Amazon gift card or check (check processing fee: $15)

- ✓ **Payout Model**: Amazon operates a volume-based advertising fee structure. The more products that are shipped as a result of your affiliate links, the more you'll make per sale, which incentivizes bloggers to refer more and more customers over time.

- ✓ **Customer Support**: Yes

- ✓ **Market Reputation**: Excellent

- ✓ **Nature of Commission**: Amazon triggers payouts only after your affiliate sales reach a minimum threshold of $10.

- ✓ **Cookie Life**: 24 hours (90 days if a referral adds a product to their shopping cart during a session you refer)

Ease of Use: Amazon offers a walkthrough for beginners. There are also many online guides available.

2. CreativeLive

CreativeLive is an online education platform where live classes are broadcasted to an international audience. The company has been operating since 2010 and has since created over two billion minutes of expert-led courses that have been viewed by millions of students from around the world. Classes range from photography and videography to arts and design, music, crafts, money and life—that are broken down into further sub-categories to make it easier for the user to find exactly what they want to learn.

- ✓ **Commission Rate**: 20% commission rate for new customer purchases, 10% for returning customer purchases and a $1 lead payout for new registrations

- ✓ **Payment Method**: Check or direct deposit

- ✓ **Payout Model**: Monthly commissions paid by ShareASale around the 22nd of the following month. Affiliates will not receive a commission check until they've earned $50 in commission.

- ✓ **Customer Support**: Yes

- ✓ **Market Reputation**: Excellent

✓ **Nature of Commission**: CPA (Cost Per Action): $1 for a new account referral and 25% Cost Per Sale (CPS) commission for new customers with 10% CPS for returning clients.

✓ **Cookie Life:** 30 days

Pros:

✓ No fees associated with the CreativeLive affiliate program

✓ Affiliates from any country can join as long as ShareASale supports their country

✓ Extra support and curated offers available for high-traffic websites

✓ You can still earn a commission on sales from a customer if they return and make a purchase within 30 days (f they didn't make a purchase initially)

✓ A range of banners, links and promotions to assist you with your marketing activities

✓ No limit/threshold to the number of links you can place on your website

Cons:

✓ No discounts available for affiliates to promote

✓ Strict coupons policy

3. Udemy

Udemy is another extremely popular online learning platform, potentially even the largest in the world. Aimed at both adults and students, thios platform has more than 30 million students and 50,000 instructors that teach courses in over 60 different languages. With over 245 million course enrollments so far, Udemy's affiliate program is an attractive choice for those who have educational blogs. The program is hosted on Rakuten LinkShare and is periodically available on other affiliate networks.

✓ **Commission Rate**: 15%

✓ **Payment Method**: Direct bank deposit

✓ **Payout Model**: Payments are made once you hit the $50 threshold

✓ **Customer Support**: Yes

✓ **Market Reputation**: Good

✓ **Nature of Commission:** You'll earn payouts for valid purchases through your affiliate tracking links and banners. The more you promote, the more you'll earn (with no caps on commissions).

✓ **Cookie Life:** 7 days

Pros:

✓ Thousands of available classes to promote on virtually ever topic imaginable (with hundreds of pre-designed banners)

✓ Deep linking opportunities

✓ Over 100+ sub-categories

✓ Promotional assets and tools available to help you drive sales

Cons:

✓ Low commissions

✓ Relatively high payout threshold ($50 minimum)

✓ Their affiliate program landing page and description could use some love

4. Survey Junkie

Survey Junkie is an online community with over 11 million users. The platform allows users to make money online and collect rewards from top brands by taking part in online surveys in their downtime. By becoming a Survey Junkie affiliate, you can earn commissions by helping drive traffic to their website. For affiliates, 100 Survey Junkie points are equal to $1 in commission. Most surveys take 1-20 minutes and are worth 10-90 points.

- ✓ **Commission Rate**: $1.50 per sign up

- ✓ **Payment Method:** PayPal

- ✓ **Payout Model:** $1.50 for every person that signs up for Survey Junkie via your affiliate link

- ✓ **Customer Support**: Yes

- ✓ **Market Reputation**: Excellent

- ✓ **Nature of Commission**: Relatively low minimum payment threshold of $10 means you can get paid frequently

- ✓ **Cookie Life:** N/A

- ✓ Ease of Use: Those who want to join the program can do so in their easy sign-up process. Commissions can be drawn via PayPal or gift card.

Pros:

✓ Reporting tools to track your campaigns

✓ Free to sign up and they give you great copy to use on your blog for highlighting their selling points to your readers

Cons:

✓ Online survey sites have traditionally gotten a bad rap, which is a real challenge in sending referrals their way

✓ Not really a con per-se, but new affiliate traffic must be of a high level of quality and they'll monitor your sign ups to ensure it's not bad leads

5. Shopify

Shopify is a Canadian-based eCommerce company that offers retail point-of-sale systems and online stores. Shopify is a complete commerce platform that lets you start, grow, and manage a business, making it the perfect option for those who are interested in starting their own drop-shipping business.

- ✓ **Commission Rate**: An average of $58 for each user who signs up for a paid plan (varies based on plan type) with your unique referral link and $2000 for each Shopify Plus referral

- ✓ **Payment Method**: PayPal

- ✓ **Payout Model:** Free to join with no monthly charges and no minimum sales requirements

- ✓ **Customer Support**: Yes

- ✓ **Market Reputation**: Excellent

- ✓ **Nature of Commission**: You can receive a 100% commission on the first and second payment, for every referral who signs up for a paid plan. Payout will occur five business days after the 15th day of the month following their sign up

- ✓ **Cookie Life**: 30 days

- ✓ **Ease of Use**: Support is available at any time via phone, email, or live chat

Pros:

✓ The affiliate program is self-hosted and uses proprietary affiliate tracking software

✓ No joining fees

✓ To maximize your earnings, each referral will be supported to help them transition from trial to paid plan

✓ Dedicated partner dashboard allows you to manage your affiliate details and track campaigns

✓ Deep linking opportunities

Cons:

✓ You will be credited with the referral only if the visitor signs up for a 14-day free trial within 30 days

6. BigCommerce

BigCommerce is another eCommerce platform that provides all the tools you need to design, maintain and scale an online store. It's one of the top eCommerce platforms in the market alongside Shopify and offers tons of built-in features and data tools to help small business owners create a powerful online store and increase their conversion rates.

- ✓ **Commission Rate**: 200% of the customer's first monthly payment and up to $1,500 per enterprise customer you refer

- ✓ **Payment Method**: Direct deposit or wire transfer

- ✓ **Payout Model**: $1.50 flat fee per lead and $40 per enterprise lead

- ✓ **Customer Support:** Yes

- ✓ **Market Reputation**: Excellent

- ✓ **Nature of Commission**: Referrals are only considered if they occur within 90 days of using your affiliate link and approved transactions are paid when they lock

- ✓ **Cookie Life**: 90 days

- ✓ **Ease of Use**: Easy to set up and monetize quickly if you've got the right content on your blog (24/7 customer support team is available too)

Pros:

- ✓ Free trial sign-up option

- ✓ High $40 commission for enterprise lead and up to $1,500 per enterprise customer that converts

- ✓ Long 90-day referral period

- ✓ Excellent customer support

Cons:

- ✓ Transactions are paid when they lock, which often takes over a month from original sign up date

7. Dreamhost

Dreamhost is consistently ranked as one of the best web hosting providers in the world, even earning the endorsement of Automattic—the makers of WordPress for their work in hosting. In addition to providing top-notch hosting plans, they also have a stellar affiliate program that pays out up to $200/sign up (depending upon the plan) and the volume of customers you're sending their way. Over time, Dreamhost has grown to become one of my best affiliate programs as my content has narrowed in on the blogging niche.

- ✓ **Commission Rate**: $15 to $200 (commission rates vary widely depending upon the plan your customer choose)

- ✓ **Payment Method**: PayPal

- ✓ **Payout Model:** Payments process 97 days after the sale (as per their 97 day money back guarantee)

- ✓ **Customer Support:** Yes

- ✓ **Market Reputation:** Excellent

- ✓ **Nature of Commission:** Affiliate payouts are processed between the 7th and 14th day of each month.

- ✓ Ease of Use: A dedicated team of affiliate managers always on call through their support channels

Pros:

- ✓ Free to join

- ✓ Very good tracking of referrals in a visual dashboard

- ✓ Applying takes just minutes

✓ No limits on how much you can earn

✓ Dedicated customer support

Cons:

✓ You have to apply and be approved in order to join the affiliate program

✓ Payments process around 97 days after each sale is complete, so there's a waiting time

8. HubSpot

HubSpot is a massive force in the marketing, sales and customer service software industries. What started originally as just a limited suite of tactical tools for marketers back in 2005, has blossomed into a publicly-traded company with well over $500 Million in annual revenue in recent years. All along though, they've maintained (and grown) an incredibly intuitive, useful set of marketing and sales tools for small business owners around the world. To top it off, they've more than earned their spot on this list of the best affiliate programs.

✓ **Commission Rate:** Starter (Basic): $250 | Professional (CMS): $500 | Enterprise: $1,000

✓ **Payment Method**: PayPal

✓ **Payout Model:** 30+ days (on the 25th of the month after the qualifying month the sale took place in)

✓ **Customer Support**: Yes

✓ **Market Reputation**: Excellent

✓ **Nature of Commission**: Payments process on the 25th day of the month after the sale took place

✓ **Cookie Life:** 90 days

✓ **Ease of Use**: HubSpot has a dedicated team of affiliate managers on staff to help at all times

Pros:

✓ Free to join

✓ Excellent tracking of referrals on a custom dashboard

✓ Signing up takes a matter of minutes

✓ No cap on how much you can earn

✓ Dedicated customer support

Cons:

- ✓ Must apply and be approved in order to join the affiliate program

- ✓ Payouts can take sometimes longer than anticipated to arrive

9. Bluehost

Bluehost is a web hosting company that's amongst the 20 largest in the world, collectively responsible for hosting over 2 million domains along with its sister companies, FastDomain, iPage and HostGator. Bluehost is ranked as having one of the best web hosting plans for bloggers who are looking for passive income opportunities on their blog (especially if their blog niche covers topics related to WordPress or writing). The company has paid out $5 million in commissions in the last year alone, making it one of the highest paying affiliate programs in web hosting.

- ✓ **Commission Rate:** $65 (with commission rate increases available based on the volume of sign ups you generate)

- ✓ **Payment Method:** PayPal

✓ **Payout Model:** Payments process between 45 and 60 days after the sale

✓ **Customer Support:** Yes

✓ **Market Reputation:** Excellent

✓ **Nature of Commission:** The payment is processed between the 16th and the last day of each month. A minimum of $100 needs to be earned for the payment to move forward.

✓ **Cookie Life:** 60 days

✓ **Ease of Use:** A dedicated team of affiliate managers always on call via email at affiliates@bluehost.com

Pros:

✓ Free to join

✓ Excellent tracking of referrals on a custom dashboard

✓ Signing up takes a matter of minutes

✓ there's no cap on how much you can earn

✓ Dedicated customer support

Cons:

✓ You have to apply and be approved in order to join the affiliate program

✓ Payments process between 45 and 60 days after each sale is complete

✓ Bluehost isn't the only company that offers great affiliate programs for their monthly hosting plans though. Consider others like Dreamhost, Namecheap and HostGator too.

10. ConvertKit

ConvertKit is one of the hottest email marketing providers that offer automation capabilities developed specifically for bloggers & creatives. The subscription-based service is focused towards bloggers, small businesses and podcasters who are looking to simplify their email marketing process. ConvertKit simplifies the process of capturing more leads and selling more of your product.

✓ **Commission Rate**: Recurring 30% commission for the lifetime of each customer you refer (paid monthly)

✓ **Payment Method:** PayPal

✓ **Payout Model:** As the accounts of each customer you refer grows, so do your payouts (all commissions are paid with a 30-day delay)

✓ **Customer Support:** Yes

✓ **Market Reputation:** Excellent

✓ **Nature of Commission:** 30% monthly recurring commission (if you refer an account with 8,000 subscribers, you'll earn $99/month)

✓ **Cookie Life:** 60 days

✓ **Ease of Use:** All you have to is enter your email address to sign up as an affiliate

Pros:

✓ No threshold to meet in order to get paid

✓ 30% monthly recurring commission (this is huge)

✓ Personalized overview dashboard gives you all the details on your earnings

Cons:

✓ 30-day delay on commission payments

11. Teachable

Teachable is a large platform that allows online teachers to host & sell their online courses on various subjects. With over 68,000 instructors and 18 million students, Teachable is one of the largest platforms of its kind, which is what makes it such a great opportunity for those who are just entering affiliate marketing.

- ✓ **Commission Rate:** Recurring 30% commission for the lifetime of each customer you refer (paid monthly)

- ✓ **Payment Method**: PayPal

- ✓ **Payout Model:** Earn a commission for as long as a customer sticks around hosting their courses on Teachable

- ✓ **Customer Support:** Yes

- ✓ **Market Reputation:** Excellent

- ✓ **Nature of Commission:** Once you refer someone, you earn a commission for as long as that person stays a customer

- ✓ **Cookie Life:** 90 days

✓ **Ease of Use:** Easy to set up and use with tons of resources and tools offered by Teachable

Pros:

✓ Join the Teachable affiliate program for free

✓ Lengthy 90-day conversion period increases your referral chances

✓ Drives up referrals with Teachable's conversion-optimized funnels

✓ Easy-access affiliate code makes it easy to earn a commission on any page

Cons:

✓ No self-referrals

✓ Referred users must stay for at least 31 days after joining in order to trigger an earned commission

12. Skillshare

Skillshare is a US-based online learning community where you can access educational courses. The subscription-based service offers access to a plethora of courses in design, photography, mobile development, web design and much more. Skillshare has become the go-to choice for millions of people around the world who are looking for personalized, on-demand educational courses.

- ✓ **Commission Rate**: $10 per sign up (one-time referral fee)

- ✓ **Payment Method**: Direct deposit

- ✓ **Payout Model:** $10 in commission for each new customer that signs up for a Premium Membership or free trial

- ✓ **Customer Support:** Yes

- ✓ **Market Reputation:** Excellent

- ✓ **Nature of Commission:** Payouts are made on or around the 16th of each month

- ✓ **Cookie Life:** 30 days

- ✓ **Ease of Use:** Easy to sign up and any affiliate-related queries can be sent to affiliates@skillshare.com

Pros:

- ✓ The affiliate program is free to join

- ✓ They have a large community of users and

brand recognition

✓ Track all your traffic, referrals and payouts with a personalized dashboard.

✓ A plethora of courses (25,000+)

✓ All sign-ups during the 14-day trial period will be counted towards your referral payouts

✓ Payouts are made on the 16th day of each month

Cons:

✓ Wide variety of course subjects can make it difficult to pinpoint the high-converting ones

13. Instapage

Instapage is a popular landing page builder that's used by marketers and eCommerce businesses around the world. Their landing page builder makes it easy to create and launch beautiful landing pages for your products or services, in order to improve sales and get more customers through the front door. The Instapage affiliate program is a great way to earn recurring income if you have an audience of marketers and eCommerce business owners on your blog.

- ✓ **Commission Rate**: 50% commission on the first payment, then 30% monthly recurring commission ongoing

- ✓ **Payment Method:** PayPal

- ✓ **Payout Model:** 50% revenue share on the first payment and 30% lifetime revenue share on all self-serve plans

- ✓ **Customer Support**: Yes

- ✓ **Market Reputation:** Great

- ✓ **Nature of Commission:** Once you receive funds, the payment will be made within a week

- ✓ **Cookie Life:** 120 days

- ✓ **Ease of Use**: Dedicated support from an account manager

Pros:

- ✓ Free to join

- ✓ Dedicated dashboard to track your progress

- ✓ Access to a vast range of promotional banners

and logos

✓ Get paid within 60 days of the sale

✓ Lengthy 120-day cookie life improves chances of getting more referrals

Cons:

✓ Commissions are canceled if the customer cancels their order within 65 days.

✓ Need to have earned at least $11.70 in order to get paid

14. FreshBooks

FreshBooks offers a very easy to use and powerful range of features that make small business accounting, invoicing and general financial management a breeze. It also removes the need for tracking any of your business financials by paper and streamlines your accounting activities, which should automatically bring down the costs of running a business. It's also a cloud-based service which means it's accessible from anywhere.

✓ **Commission Rate**: $5 per free trial signup plus $55 per paid subscription

✓ **Payment Method:** Direct deposit (via ShareASale where their program is hosted)

✓ **Payout Model:** $5 per free trial signup plus $55 per paid subscriber (top performers unlock bonus commission offers)

✓ **Customer Support**: Yes

✓ **Market Reputation**: Excellent

✓ **Nature of Commission**: Payment schedule is handled by ShareASale (and need to reach a minimum of $50 before they can be transferred to your account)

✓ **Cookie Life:** 120 days

✓ **Ease of Use:** Very easy to find and get set up in ShareASale (dedicated in-house support is available at affiliates@freshbooks.com)

Pros:

✓ Free sign up

✓ Extended 120 days cookie tracking

✓ Poaching protection improves your chances of getting more referrals

✓ Lots of beautiful landing pages you can use in your promotions to drive traffic towards

Cons:

✓ All referring links need to be verifiable

✓ No coupon, rewards or loyalty websites allowed

15. Adobe

Adobe is a US-based multinational computer software company that offers a suite of creative and multimedia products. With a revenue-generating capacity of $9.03 billion, it's easy to see why joining Adobe's Affiliate Program is an attractive opportunity for many budding bloggers. Currently, bloggers can promote Adobe products like their Adobe Creative Cloud (which includes Photoshop, Illustrator & InDesign), Adobe Stock and Adobe Document Cloud to earn commissions.

✓ **Commission Rate:**

✓ **Payment Method:** Direct deposit

✓ **Payout Model:** Payments for the first month on monthly and yearly subscriptions

✓ **Customer Support:** Yes

✓ **Market Reputation:** Excellent

✓ **Nature of Commission:** Month-to-Month subscription: 85% of the first month. One Year, prepaid subscription: 8.33% of the first-year payment

✓ **Cookie Life:** 30 days

✓ **Ease of Use:** Slightly more complex to get set up and optimized. All questions can be sent to adobeaffiliates@arvato.com

Pros:

✓ Access to a comprehensive selection of ready-to-publish marketing banners and text links

✓ Up-to-date information on new product launches

✓ Regular and exclusive promotions for added income

✓ Dedicated Adobe Affiliates dashboard

✓ Deep linking opportunities

Cons:

✓ Document cloud and Stock are only available to promote in specific countries

16. FlexJobs

FlexJobs is an online portal that offers a plethora of job listings. It's a valuable resource for those who are looking for jobs quickly. Many of the job listings on FlexJobs offer remote flexibility, making it one of the best remote jobs websites on the market. Job listings on the site are also broken down into categories, which makes it easier to find a particular job with relative ease.

✓ **Commission Rate**: Up to $15 for each paid subscription you refer

✓ **Payment Method:** PayPal

✓ **Payout Model:** Get paid monthly for the commissions generated in your previous month

✓ **Customer Support:** Yes

✓ **Market Reputation:** Excellent

✓ **Nature   of   Commission:**   Earn

commissions for referring job seekers to a paid FlexJobs premium account

✓ **Cookie Life:** N/A

✓ **Ease of Use:** You can find the FlexJobs affiliate program on many affiliate networks, but their own internal program (located here) pays out the highest commission rates

Pros:

✓ No cap on commissions

✓ FlexJobs scores very well compared to other brands in the job search industry which makes them a good choice for affiliate marketing opportunities

Cons:

✓ Requires you to apply and fill out a questionnaire in order to be approved for the affiliate program

17. SolidGigs

SolidGigs simplifies the search process for freelance job seekers by sending you the best 2% of freelance gigs every week. The subscription-based service makes it easier for freelancers to find a broad range of income opportunities without having to do all the legwork of new client outreach all the time.

- ✓ **Commission Rate**: 35% commission of each new paid sign up you refer

- ✓ Payment Method: PayPal

- ✓ **Payout Model:** Cost-Per-Sale

- ✓ **Customer Support:** Yes

- ✓ **Market Reputation:** Excellent

- ✓ **Nature of Commission**: One-time payment for the referral of new customers (accumulated and paid out to affiliates each month)

- ✓ **Cookie Life**: 30 days

- ✓ **Ease of Use:** Currently an invite-only affiliate program that's run by SolidGigs and Millo.co founder Preston Lee (you can email him at preston@millo.co)

Pros:

- ✓ Great internal affiliate tracking system that gives you clear data on your referrals (and conversion rates)

✓ Library of creative assets to get your promotions started

Cons:

✓ Privately run program, so you'll likely need to have an existing audience of freelancers in order to be approved to join

18.Bonsai

Bonsai is one of the highest-rated online business management software providers for freelancers. They offer an all-in-one suite of tools that help freelancers and solopreneurs work together, streamline project management, collect payments and deliver invoices. Since the world is moving towards a gig economy, platforms like Bonsai will be very valuable moving forward, which is why this makes a great choice for bloggers who reach freelancers and small business owners. Affiliates also get to take advantage of cash bonuses, increased payouts and exclusive discounts for top performers.

✓ **Commission Rate**: 25% commission on each paid subscription sign up you refer

✓ **Payment Method:** PayPal or direct

deposit

- ✓ **Payout Model:** 25% commission on paid subscriptions

- ✓ **Customer Support**: Yes

- ✓ **Market Reputation**: Excellent

- ✓ **Nature of Commission**: You'll earn a monthly commission for the first 12 months of each paid plan you refer (if someone subscribes to the $29 plan you get $7.25 /mo for a full 12 months)

- ✓ **Cookie Life:** N/A

- ✓ **Ease of Use:** Very easy to sign up and get to promoting (questions can be sent to the Bonsai team at support@hellobonsai.com)

Pros:

- ✓ 25% monthly commission for 12 months on each paid plan is pretty great

- ✓ Cash bonus for writing about them on your blog, increased payout options and exclusive discounts for top performers

Cons:

✓ Their landing pages could use some work in order to convert better

19. Contena

Contena is both a freelance job board and a freelance training academy. This subscription-based service, while only a few years old, has garnered a lot of traction lately because of its high-quality freelance job listings and training academy that guides new freelancers through the process of becoming successful as a contract worker. The combination of a job board, training, tools and coaching makes this platform a pretty great resource, especially for freelance writers.

✓ **Commission Rate:** Up to $200 per paid membership you refer (varies based on products and plans)

✓ **Payment Method**: PayPal

✓ **Payout Model:** Cost-Per-Sale

✓ **Customer Support:** Yes

✓ **Market Reputation**: Great

✓ **Nature of Commission**: You'll earn a payout for customers you refer after they purchase a training program from Contena

✓ **Cookie Life:** N/A

✓ **Ease of Use:** Their sign up process is a bit of a black box (after submitting the Google Doc with info about your blog, you'll have to wait until hearing back)

20. Kinsta

Kinsta offers the best cloud-based hosting for WordPress bloggers, hands down (they power my blog here). Utilizing Google Cloud and LXD orchestrated Linux containers under the hood at their data centers around the world, Kinsta is widely considered to be one of the best managed hosting providers available for bloggers. The company has a reputation of providing lightning fast hosting, SSL support via Let's Encrypt for added protection, optimized backups and hassle-free migration amongst many other features.

✓ **Commission Rate:** Earn up to $500 for every referral (depending upon plan value) + 10% monthly recurring lifetime commissions

✓ **Payment Method:** Via PayPal

✓ **Payout Model:** Signup bonus + 10% recurring

✓ **Customer Support:** Yes

✓ **Market Reputation:** Excellent

✓ **Nature of Commission**: Earnings are paid in a 60-day conversion window

✓ **Cookie Life:** 60 days

✓ **Ease of Use:** Very easy to apply and get started (you can contact the affiliate manager directly at affiliates@kinsta.com)

Pros:

✓ Real-time tracking on a customized multilingual affiliate dashboard

✓ 60 day conversion window

✓ Create your unique affiliate link with a single click and point it anywhere on the Kinsta website

✓ Quick promotional materials and banners

Cons:

✓ Affiliates are not allowed to take part in any incentivized programs, business opportunity sites or post links to Kinsta (whether a referral link or not) on coupon sites

✓ Affiliates are only allowed to use advertising materials promoting Kinsta that are approved by Kinsta

21.OptimizePress

OptimizePress hails itself as the first and best landing page builder for WordPress, which I've used on my blog for 5+ years. Their 3-in-1 toolkit makes it easy for marketers to build beautiful landing pages, sales pages and membership sites to help elevate the value of their content. OptimizePress is ideal for promoting your backend funnel if you sell eBooks, digital products, online courses, events and manage other digital revenue streams.

✓ **Commission Rate:** 40% per sale on front end sales (up to $118.80) + 20% recurring on all club subscription sales.

✓ **Payment Method:** PayPal

✓ **Payout Model:** OptimizePress operates a customer only affiliate program (to join this program, you need an active OptimizePress account)

✓ **Customer Support:** Yes

✓ **Nature of Commission:** You need 2 sales before commissions are paid and a minimum of $100 due in commissions to trigger a commission payout

✓ **Market Reputation:** Excellent

✓ **Cookie Life:** 180 days

✓ **Ease of Use:** Uses an industry-leading FirstPromotor system for managing their affiliate program (affiliates also get access to their own stats dashboard to track affiliate referrals and generate tracking links)

Pros:

✓ 40% commission is paid on referred sales of the OptimizePress Core, Publisher and Pro packages

✓ PPC campaigners can bid on any keywords (including product names)

✓ Affiliates are paid monthly (around the 1st of

each month)

Cons:

- ✓ Purchasing through your own link is strictly prohibited

- ✓ Payments are only sent when orders have been finalized (passed their 30 day guarantee period)

- ✓ Not permitted to use any domain names containing the words OptimizePress, OptimizePress 2, OptimizePress, James Dyson, dyson, dison, BusinessJolt, businessjolt, or business jolt

- ✓ All balances on dormant accounts are cleared after 365 days of no earnings

22. SEMRush

SEMrush is a trusted source for SEO tools that help online businesses and marketers with their keyword research, tracking and search engine optimization. The tools offered by SEMrush come highly recommended for improving the ranking of your website by doing more effective keyword research. Their affiliate program is a great option for bloggers to earn a recurring income via BeRush (SEMRush's exclusive affiliate program).

- ✓ Commission Rate: 40%

- ✓ Payment Method: PayPal or direct transfer

- ✓ Payout Model: 40% commission from sales of all SEMrush plans (Pro, Guru, Business)

- ✓ Customer Support: Yes

- ✓ Market Reputation: Excellent

- ✓ Nature of Commission: BeRush is a partnership based on revenue sharing, where the affiliate (you) promotes SEMrush in exchange for a commission of every sale

- ✓ Cookie Life: 10 years

- ✓ Ease of Use: Online customer support available

Pros:

- ✓ Variety of promo materials in 7 languages

- ✓ Each month the BeRush team runs the BeRush Contest where participants can win up to $100 for the best content

- ✓ Commission payments made up to twice a

month

✓ Exclusive promotional rights to one of the world's leading competitive intelligence services

Cons:

✓ Account balance needs to reach $50 or more to get paid

✓ No payments are made for referring existing or returning SEMrush users

23. Interact

Interact is an online tool that's used for creating quizzes with the goal of engaging your readers and generating more leads. Their tools can also be used to segment a brand's audience and help drive traffic to a website. Quizzes are turning out to be a fun way for marketers to attract their audience and keep things interesting with their audience, making this a great program to participate in. Whether it's scored quizzes, assessment quizzes, or personality quizzes, Interact's library makes it easy to create attractive quizzes on-the-fly with its 800+ pre-made templates, tools and much more.

✓ **Commission Rate**: 30% monthly recurring (for the lifetime of each customer)

✓ **Payment Method:** PayPal or Stripe

✓ **Payout Model:** You can earn commissions for every month that your qualifying customers subscribe to the platform

✓ **Customer Support:** Yes

✓ **Market Reputation:** Great

✓ **Nature of Commission:** Payments for sales are issued once a month through a payout method of your choice (you must have at least $25 in rewards in order to cash out)

✓ **Cookie Life:** N/A

✓ **Ease of Use:** Easy to use and set up

Pros:

✓ Dedicated affiliate dashboard to track your referrals

✓ PartnerStack helps give you the tools and resources you need to promote our product

✓ Payments are verified and paid-out the

month after your commission is earned.

Cons:

✓ Application reviewing time can take a while
to get approved

24. WP Engine

Another giant in the web hosting space, WP Engine
has been around since 2010 when they launched
into the industry as a premium-positioned
WordPress hosting provider that focused on the
niche of selling lightning fast hosting plans to
established bloggers, businesses and companies
that need reliable hosting. They've also got one of
the best affiliate programs on the market for
bloggers that cover web hosting related topics.

✓ **Commission Rate:** $200 minimum
commissions for WP Engine sales and 35%
of StudioPress theme sales

✓ **Payment Method:** PayPal or ACH

✓ **Payout Model:** Earn a commission for
every new customer you refer to WP Engine
or StudioPress

✓ **Customer Support:** Yes

✓ **Market Reputation:** Great

✓ **Nature of Commission:** Payouts vary based on the plan your referred customer signs up for

✓ **Cookie Life:** 180 days

✓ **Ease of Use:** Easy to use and get set up

Pros:

✓ Dedicated affiliate dashboard to track your referrals

✓ Team of affiliate managers standing by for any questions

✓ The ability to create custom landing pages with the WP Engine design team

Cons:

✓ You must apply to join the affiliate program before being accepted

25. IP Vanish

IPVanish is an industry leading VPN provider that delivers the best VPN speeds, the most secure connections and the most competitive pricing anywhere. This VPN offers a secure solution to protect online activity and personal information (and one of the best affiliate programs for bloggers too). Their network spans 40,000+ IPs on 1,300+ servers in 75+ locations, giving you the ability to surf anonymously and access blocked websites from every corner of the globe.

- ✓ **Commission Rate:** 1-month package: 100%, then 35% recurring. 3-month package: 40%, then 35% recurring.1 & 2 year package: 40%, then 30% recurring

- ✓ **Payment Method:** Paypal

- ✓ **Payout Model:** Payments are made once you hit the $100 threshold

- ✓ **Customer Support:** Yes

- ✓ **Market Reputation:** Excellent

- ✓ **Nature of Commission:** You'll earn payouts for valid purchases that do not cancel within the first month. Earn a commission of 100% of first month's revenue, and 30% every month that customer sticks around

- ✓ **Cookie Life:** 14 days

✓ **Ease of Use:** Easy to sign up on their private affiliate platform. Great affiliate support available from Dustin Howes and the affiliate team at support@affiliategroove.com

Pros:

✓ Highest industry payouts in a high volume security industry

✓ Consistently updating latest coupons

✓ Great conversion rates at 9%<

✓ Average order value at $40+

✓ Helpful affiliate managers ready to help you succeed

Cons:

✓ Highly competitive field

✓ High payout threshold ($100 minimum)

✓ On private network (Post Affiliate Pro), with limited reporting

26. Affluent

Tired of logging in to a dozen affiliate management tools just to see how your affiliate campaigns are performing? Affluent aggregates all your affiliate data into a single dashboard, then lets you decide how you want to view that data—making it the best way I've found to keep a close pulse on your affiliate performance all in one destination. Log into their platform to see all your links, reports and program alerts. This is a major time saver and a powerful organizational tool for affiliates that are managing memberships in many programs at once.

- ✓ **Commission Rate:** 100% of first month's revenue, Two-tier Commission: 20% for every sale of affiliates you recruited

- ✓ **Payment Method:** Check or direct deposit

- ✓ **Payout Model:** Monthly commissions paid out by ShareASale around the 22nd of the following month. Affiliates will not receive a commission check until they've earned $50 in commission.

- ✓ **Customer Support:** Yes

- ✓ **Market Reputation:** Great

- ✓ **Nature of Commission:** You'll earn

payouts for valid purchases that do not cancel within the first month. Earn a commission of 100% of first month's revenue. Recruit a friend to the affiliate program and earn 20% of all of their sales.

✓ **Cookie Life:** 180 days

✓ **Ease of Use:** Very easy to get set up in ShareASale (dedicated in-house support is available at affiliates@affluent.io)

Pros:

✓ A unique product that every affiliate should know about and use

✓ Generous payouts and average order value at $60+

✓ Offer free trial and 180 cookie duration to maximize conversion opportunity

✓ Helpful affiliate managers ready to help you succeed

Cons:

✓ Smaller brand

✓ No coupon, rewards or loyalty websites allowed

✓ Limited marketing assets (landing pages and banners)

There you have it. These are my top picks for affiliate programs that bloggers should prioritize joining to increase their affiliate income this year.

Most of these affiliate programs for bloggers have a low barrier of entry too, so they should be relatively quick & easy to sign up for—even if you're a relatively new blogger just starting your blog.

Chapter Four
Easy Way Affiliate Marketing Can Completly Transform Your Blog

An affiliate program is a marketing tactic that allows you to get paid for promoting someone else's product or service on your website (Need to build a website still? Check out my list of the best website builders for bloggers today) . You're paid a commission each time one of your readers clicks through to the advertiser's site and makes a purchase or fulfills a specified conversion (like a sign-up form or email capture).

Affiliate marketing is beneficial for all involved:

1. The web visitor: The audience member who clicks through to the advertiser's website is exposed or reintroduced to a brand they may have never heard of otherwise.

2. The advertiser: The company or person who receives the added traffic and potential increased sales can reach a completely new

audience.

3. The affiliate (you): You get to showcase products and brands in your blog niche you love with your readers, improving their lives and building your side income.

But does it work? If you need proof that affiliate marketing for bloggers is a revenue generator, check out these statistics:

Affiliate network participation from content publishers increased 175% over the past two years. Developed affiliate programs account for generating 15 to 30% of all advertisers' online sales. Affiliate marketing sales revenue driven by content publishers increased 240% over the past two years.

In 2017, $5.3 billion was spent on affiliate marketing. This number is expected to grow 10.1% each year until 2020, where spend will reach $6.8 billion.

How Effective Is Affiliate Marketing?

Brands recognize the value of affiliate marketing, and that's evident through digital spending. As of 2016, 81% of brands and 84% of publishers leverage affiliate marketing. While there's money to be made in virtually any niche, affiliate marketing is most popular among fashion, sports, and health and wellness brands.

A study of 550 affiliate marketing programs revealed 18.7 percent of affiliate campaigns promoted fashion products, 14.6 percent were associated with affiliate marketing for sports and outdoor products, and health/wellness and beauty accounted for 11.1 percent.

Affiliate marketing for bloggers is most effective when you, the blogger, have a strong audience that relies on you for trustworthy information. Building your audience is a key component to success (and passive income) through affiliate marketing.

Take DudePerfect for example. A group of five friends challenging each other to nail the perfect trick basketball shot turned into a mega YouTube channel and tons of brands vying for the guys to promote their product.

How Do Affiliate Marketing Bloggers Get Paid?

Affiliate marketing bloggers can get paid in different ways, based on different performance factors. The three most common ways to earn money through affiliate marketing are:

✓ **Pay per sale:** This is a commission-based

payment method where you earn a set commission based on each sale that comes from a referral visitor from your website. The more sales you generate for the merchant, the more money you make.

✓ Pay per lead: Merchants pay you each time you bring a lead to the company. This method is used when a user signs up for a program of some sort a trial, demo, newsletter, etc.

✓ **Pay per click:** Click-through affiliate marketing pays you each time a visitor clicks on the merchant's ad that's on your blog. However, not each click converts to a sale and can become quite expensive, so the pay-per-click method is rarely offered by merchants.

How To (Quickly) Grow A Blog Audience

Before you can make money with affiliate marketing, you need to grow your blog audience. And just creating a blog isn't enough to build an audience of loyal readers. You need traffic!

If your blog is brand new, it will take some time before you get enough traffic to monetize your site with affiliate links. However, you should keep affiliate products that you want to promote in the back of your mind when developing your content strategy.

You'll need to incorporate a number of tactics that have the potential to increase your reader base, outlined below.

1. Publish Outstanding Content.

It's very simple if your content isn't that good or can be found somewhere else, your blog will not be successful. Period. Do not simply post an article because it's Wednesday and some "guru" says you should blog mid-week. Say something valuable. Give your readers something they can use so they leave your blog feeling more enlightened than when they arrived. To stay relevant with your readers:

✓ Monitor trending content. By staying at the forefront of what's being discussed and searched online, you can write to the demand of online users.

✓ Use Google Alerts as a tool that indicates what people are searching and consuming.

✓ Rely on tools like Buzzsumo to know who and what is making an impact in your niche.

✓ Understand your competitor's strategy.

When you're competing for traffic and customers, use SEMrush and Ahrefs for insight into your competitor's keyword ranking.

2. Engage with Other Bloggers.

Make the most of your decision to create a website and begin blogging—forge mutual connections with other bloggers by reaching out and engaging with them on social media, email, or face-to-face communication if possible. Share or comment on their social posts. Leave comments on their blogs. The key is to provide value! If you can, help with link building, guest posts contributions, door social shares. If you can show that you're a valuable resource, they may help you in the future.

3. Become a Contributor.

Find the top blogs in your niche and submit your pieces to be posted as a guest blogger. If possible, introduce yourself and get to know the blogger before sending your pitch to increase your likelihood of being picked up. There are a number of cold email templates you can use to start a conversation. Guest blogging will help increase awareness about your blog, but you also need to include an author bio (typically positioned at the bottom of the blog) with a link connecting readers to your website or an opt-in page to receive an email when you post new blogs.

4. Perform Keyword Research.

Ah keyword research. Although your blog posts should focus on a very specific niche and web of related topics, you need to know how well these articles can potentially rank on Google. Use a tool like Google Keyword Planner to view your target keyword's monthly search volume and competitive metrics when deciding on blog titles. Remember, the target keyword should be used in your META title and throughout your body copy.

A great SEO tactic is to do create one "featured article" where you send all guest post and link building traffic. This post will be the cornerstone of your website and you should focus on getting as many links as possible to this URL. Aim for a target keyword here with 25,000+ searches/month on Google and make sure to shorten the blog URL to only include the focus keyword. For example, Ryan's amazing post "10 Steps: How to Start a Blog on the Side and Make Money in 2018 (The Ultimate Guide)" simply has the URL ending in /how-start-blog/ (and is dominating search engines).

5. Get Social.

Make it easy for readers to share your content directly from your blog with social media share icons. If you're a social media star and your content is highly shared, use the shared number tool, so readers will know when 1K+ others have shared your content to Facebook, LinkedIn, or other platforms. Place the buttons before, after, or floating to the side of your content for the most use.

Once you build a solid audience through your blog and social content, you have more validity with advertisers and will be able to join more affiliate programs.

Affiliate Marketing Basics: How To Promote Products

Congratulations! You've developed your blog content and are generating some serious traffic you can now begin to monetize your blog with affiliate links. Once you sign on with affiliate marketing programs, don't think throwing up a few banner ads will allow you to rake in the cash. It takes skill, effort, an intuitive affiliate tracker and at times— reevaluation to turn affiliate marketing blogging into a steady income.

Before we delve into the different ways you can

promote a product on your blog, let's consider how you first find the best products for affiliate marketing.

1. Know Your Audience.

You must know who your core audience is before you can select products to promote through affiliate marketing. Who is your ideal reader? Why do they consume your content? What do they do on a sunny Saturday afternoon? Do they prefer Seinfeld or Friends (I will judge their answer)? To be effective you need to play the room and understand your audience's pain points.

If your blog is about the latest tech gadgets and you're promoting camping supplies, you're not only going to miss the mark, but you're likely to lose the trust of your audience. Choose products you know your audience will love and can address a problem they have.

2. Specify Your Niche.

Once you have a firm understanding of your audience, dive into your blog niche even further. For a healthy cooking blog, explore which brands coincide with your philosophies. Will you only support brands that use natural ingredients, are vegan-friendly, biodynamic (whatever that means), or responsibly sourced? Decide what principles you'll follow to determine the best products for affiliate marketing through your blog.

Connect with your readers on a regular basis. Choose 10 random email subscribers each month and request a meeting with them. Interview them and learn their pain points. The further you dive into your niche and understand the problems you're solving, the more successful your content will be, and the more money you will make with affiliate marketing.

3. You Need to Actually Use the Product.

If you don't know this by now, please be aware that your audience can sniff out a BS blog post faster than you can hit them with a sexy retargeting campaign. If you wouldn't use the product or you don't completely understand how it works, what it does, or the brand that makes it, do not promote it. Period. The fastest way to lose readers is to produce content that's clearly only created for the cash.

When you know your readers, understand the brands in your niche that match your principles, and have used the product to know you fully support it, it's time to promote.

Bloggers can use affiliate links in a number of ways. Banner ads above, below, and throughout your blog are a common method of affiliate marketing.

However, you're a writer, so the most natural way for you to promote a product is through your words. As you write about certain brands or products, you'll link back to the merchant's website for that particular item with contextual text links. The link will be traced by an affiliate marketing program, and when the online user makes a purchase or completes the conversion, you get a commission based on the cookie duration usually 30-90 days. Simple, right?

Affiliate marketing isn't a complex concept, but it takes a dedicated, consistent blogger to reach the full revenue potential. Which brings us to our next point: How do you get paid through affiliate marketing?

4. Place Your Affiliate Links in the Right Places to Maximize Impact (and Clicks).

There are a number of different ways a blogger can drive sales through their affiliate links. The most common is text links in blog posts themselves. When writing content about a product you want to promote, place text links in the product titles to send traffic to the merchant's website. Each merchant also has a specific cookie duration, so you can get credit for a sale 30, 60, or even 90 days after the click takes place.

One of the most important strategies a blogger can participate in is creating an email list. And once you have this list of loyal readers, you should place affiliate links inside of your email content. Better yet, you should have a welcome email series that builds trust with your audience and eventually links to the products you want to promote. But don't get spammy with your email links. Make sure to provide excellent and useful content first, then sprinkle in a few affiliate links to the main products you want to promote in later emails in the series.

If you're a vlogger that wants to take part in affiliate marketing, you can place affiliate links in your video descriptions, or even in the video overlays that lay on top of your videos. Product review videos are a great way to engage with your audience, provide more valuable information than you can in a simple blog post, and generate affiliate sales on places like YouTube.

10 Ways Affiliate Marketing Will Transform Your Blog (and Side Income)

Now that we've covered the basics, it's time to ramp up your affiliate marketing strategies. If you want to make extra cash without putting too much thought into it or you want to ramp up your blog to be able to quit your day job, here are the 10 ways affiliate marketing will transform your blog.

1. Build a Loyal Community.

By picking the right products and services to sell on your blog, you build your readers' trust. Your audience gets used to the idea of taking your advice and buying the products you recommend. As we touched on earlier, your relationship with your audience is the most important asset you can bring to the table as an affiliate. While your content will get people to your site, your community will get them to stay.

2. Optimize Your Conversion Rates.

Taking part in affiliate marketing will force you to examine your blog's conversion rates. Let's say you are promoting a specific product via affiliate links on a landing page. If you currently get 1,000 visits/month at a 3% conversion rate, you have 30 referrals. To get to 60 referrals, you either have to get 1,000 more visitors to the page with blogging, SEO efforts, paid traffic or social media marketing. Or you could simply increase the conversion rate to 6%.

Which one sounds easier to you? Instead of spending all of your time and effort to get new traffic, you just have to optimize the traffic you already have. Optimizing your conversion rate can include testing your calls-to-action, testing your copy, editing your UX, color schemes, and page layouts to maximize impact. By doing some simple A/B testing and optimizing your landing pages, you'll get quicker results with much less work.

3. Discover New Products.

As an affiliate marketing blogger, you'll develop an eye for new products and services that hit the market in your niche. Whether it comes at the recommendation of an affiliate program or a fellow blogger, new products will emerge that make your life better (and you get to share that with your audience). Check out these affiliate programs if you're on the hunt for good affiliate products:

- ✓ Amazon Associates
- ✓ ClickBank
- ✓ Rakuten
- ✓ ShareASale

4. Build Relationships with Merchants.

Merchants want affiliates to promote their products, and they most likely have a number of different commission rates based on the volume of traffic the affiliate generates and their current relationship with them. Once you join a merchant's affiliate program and have a few sales under your belt, reach out to the person who manages their program and set up a quick introductory meeting.

During this meeting, tell the merchant how much you enjoy promoting their product, ask them about their highest converting landing pages, and see what commission bumps you could expect to receive to promote them more on your site. This simple conversation could result in a commission bump resulting in getting 2x more revenue from each sale that you create for them.

Building real relationships with merchants is a fast way to improve your blog's sales funnel, understand the products you're promoting better, make more per sale, and even get some free products.

5. Stay Ahead of Trends and Emerging Brands.

As an active blogger, you'll be among the first to see emerging brands in your niche. When you're one of the first affiliate marketing bloggers to get behind a brand (that aligns with your personal principles and you actually use), you become a trusted voice of authority on the product or service.

When you use the appropriate SEO terms, you'll also gain traction with Google, which looks favorably on unique content. By blogging about brands that have just hit the scene, you're not competing with as many content-driven sites, improving your SERP ranking for your target keywords.

6. Take on Guest Bloggers.

Marketers who prioritize blogging efforts are 13x more likely to see positive ROI, but those blogging efforts don't have to come just from you. As you build your trust with readers, you have an opportunity to partner with guest bloggers.

The good news is, the majority of bloggers are eager to guest post or have you post to their sites. Curata says 57 percent of business bloggers outsourced blog posts from contributed or guest posts. Use your available resources to offer a change to your readers and make connections with other affiliate marketing bloggers.

7. Promote Products You Don't Have to Create.

It's much easier to promote a product that already exists than it is to create something from scratch, educate the consumer, and launch a marketing campaign. By utilizing an affiliate program, you avoid the hassles of product development, launching, and inventory. Your focus is on a product or service that works well for you—not finding storage space for the latest gadget you created or trying to code an update to a software tool.

No cost of goods, no shipping fees, and no overhead means you can give your customers instant access to what they want.

Over time, you can work on your own info product or online course to provide your readers, but affiliate marketing is a revenue stream that can make an instant impact without too much work up front.

8. Increase Brand Awareness.

While you're promoting certain products through affiliate marketing, you also get your blog in front of a larger audience. With the additional traffic generated through Google searches about an affiliate product, your personal brand awareness increases.

By building brand awareness, you can also increase your market share. Building an audience through brand awareness is more valuable than direct sales for more than 70 percent of brand managers. Your audience begins to recognize you as the go-to for information they can use in your specific niche. Whether it's a product review, life hack, or best way to post to social media, your audience increases in size because your brand is being seen by some who otherwise wouldn't have visited your blog.

9. Open the Door for a Second Blog or Podcast.

Affiliate marketing revenue can be used to go into other online ventures. Managing multiple blogs has a number of benefits. Your first blog is likely an experiment that may not work perfectly—a completely natural part of the trial and error process. The second (or third) blog can be a culmination of all that you've learned from your first efforts.

While a second blog does call for a unique niche and voice (otherwise why do it?), it expands your reach into different target audiences. Expanding into multiple blogs also allows you to keep your first blog "pure" of crossover that wouldn't fit well with your audience or goals.

You could also take your affiliate earnings and start a podcast that takes the content from your blog and repackages it into an audio format. The initial funds could be used for audio equipment and marketing your new show.

Rather than promoting outside your niche, you've now learned enough along the way to create a new platform for your message.

10. Monetize Your Email Subscribers.

Positioning yourself as an expert in your niche and promoting products through affiliate programs means readers depend on you for regular email updates with valuable information.

They'll want to know about new products you're using (like the hottest travel backpacks on the market this year if you're a travel blogger or teach people how to land travel jobs), your thoughts on certain brands if you're an influencer in your space—and read your reviews so that they can make more informed decisions.

By incorporating an email sign-up within your blog posts, in website pop-ups, sidebars, and on your homepage, you can grow your email marketing database. Once users have signed up for your email list, treat your email list like a CRM. You can send an automated welcome series that will guide users on a specific journey, with the end goal of monetization.

Your first welcome email should thank the reader for subscribing, discuss their specific pain point (and how you have felt it yourself), and develop a narrative around solving the problem. Once you've developed a rapport, further emails can include affiliate links, which will monetize your emails quickly and efficiently, without the need for your own info product or online course—though you could eventually expand into selling your own white-labeled products to increase margins like the Pure Optical team has done.

The return on email marketing is well worth the time spent. For every $1 you spend on email marketing, you can expect an average return of $38. So don't limit your affiliate marketing to just blog content, you can utilize newsletters and email blasts to stay engaged with your readers and make even more money.

Affiliate marketing is one of the absolute best ways to make money online with your blog, but in order to be successful and build yourself as an authority in your niche, you must create valuable content and build a relationship with your audience. Monetizing your blog through affiliate marketing can help grow your reach while creating a lucrative and evergreen revenue source.

I hope that by using a few of these affiliate marketing tips, you get a tiny bit closer to realizing your dreams. Whether it's generating a passive income and traveling the world, making some side cash so you can spend more time with your family, or just delivering your message to the world, I want you to be successful.

Chapter Five
Best Niches To Choose When Planning To Start A Blog To Make Money

It's already a steep climb to support yourself with a blog. There are thousands of them on the internet, which makes competing as a professional blogger difficult. Choosing one of the best blog niches for your needs can give you a head start.

By creating content related to the most popular and profitable subject matter, you can increase the chances you'll establish a following and also have monetization opportunities. If you're hoping to blog for a living, these aspects are key.

In this chapter, we'll explore what niches are and how they fit into the blogging industry. Then we'll take a closer look at some of the best blog niches to choose from.

Understanding niches and why they're important for blogging

In blogging, a niche is typically thought of as a specific area in which a blogger specializes. Their content relates to this particular subject matter and is considered high-quality and authoritative on the topic.

Not every blog has a niche, and there is some debate over whether or not a blog must stick to a specific niche in order to be successful. However, it is generally acknowledged that niches provide some useful qualities to blog sites.

First, a niche focuses your blog's content. If you decide to just write about any subject that comes to mind, your blog can become somewhat chaotic. Visitors may not be able to make sense of what your blog is 'about,' and this can impact your retention rates.

Scattered subject matter also makes it more difficult to build a dedicated audience. Visitors typically make their way to blogs looking for information on a certain topic. If your blog covers many areas, it will be harder to encourage first-time readers to engage with additional posts that may not be relevant to their interests.

Finally, sticking to a niche can help establish your credibility. Writing in-depth about one or a few topics gives you the chance to demonstrate your knowledge, while writing broadly and shallowly usually isn't very impressive.

Should you choose to pursue a specific niche, the decision isn't one to make lightly. You'll likely be working in this area for years, so you want your subject to be something you find interesting and enjoyable. However, it also helps if it already has an established audience and opportunities for profit.

There's a host of potential blogging niches available for hobbyists and professionals alike. Many – if not all – of them can be profitable. High-quality content and strong Search Engine Optimization (SEO) are more critical for a blog's success than a niche.

Even so, the blogging niches below tend to give adoptees a higher likelihood of being able to live comfortably off their blog's revenue. We've compiled this list by looking into which niches tend to receive the most traffic and generate the most income.

1. Food

Everyone eats, so naturally, food is a popular blogging topic. You can gain a fair amount of organic traffic through recipe posts, and you also have the potential to branch out into cookbooks and tutorials. Plus, according to income reports, there are plenty of food blogs raking in thousands each month.

You have an even better chance of crafting a successful blog if you choose to specialize in a particular diet. Vegan and vegetarian blogs, for example, have an easier time building a loyal audience than more generalized food blogs, as do blogs related to specific food allergies.

2. Fashion

Fashion blogs are one of the most searched-for types of blogs on the web. Should you choose to start one, there's a fairly good chance you'll be able to bring in organic traffic fairly quickly since thousands of people are looking to follow new blogs in this niche:

There are also many opportunities for sponsorships since working with products is built into the subject matter. You could also easily expand your brand onto other platforms such as Instagram and YouTube, creating additional revenue streams.

3. Personal Finance

Managing your money can be pretty confusing, which might be why so many people turn to personal finance blogs for help. And, since they tend to be run by finance-savvy individuals, perhaps it's not surprising that there are quite a few of these blogs making tens or even hundreds of thousands of dollars per month:

This is a niche that isn't easy to just jump into. While you don't necessarily need formal finance-related education, you'll at least want to have a good handle on your own money, and tips and tricks you can share with readers.

4. Lifestyle

The 'lifestyle' blogging niche is a bit of a catch-all. It only requires bloggers to write about their daily lives and related topics, so lifestyle blogs don't always stick as closely to a single topic as those in some other niches.

An entire industry has sprung up around this niche, with vast opportunities for sponsorships and other monetization techniques. The biggest challenge will likely be finding ways to stand out from the crowd in order to gain the visibility needed to grow your readership.

5. Blogging

As strange as it may initially seem to put "blogging" on a list of the best blog niches, blogging is actually a fairly popular topic for blogs. When you think about it though, it starts to make a little more sense. Most people get into blogging because they enjoy it, so it follows that they'd like to write about the subject as well:

Plus, when you're already tapped into the blogging community, other blogs are an obvious resource for advice and news. This might help explain why there are blogs in this niche that see more than 100,000 visitors come in through organic search.

How to Make Money

This is the obvious one. The real elephant in the room.

Many beginning bloggers often find themselves asking if they need to start a blog on making money to make any money.

It's a great question because all of the blogs that teach you how to make money seem to be run by people that only make money through those types of blogs. Luckily, this isn't the only niche that can do well with making money but it's one of the easiest...

Too many bloggers jump into this niche and take the wrong approach. They pretend that they have the knowledge to share with others about making money online but this audience isn't stupid.

They know they have other options so if you can't show them in some way that you know what you are talking about then you won't be making the type of money you thought. So does this mean that beginning bloggers can't enter this niche? Of course not.

The way I would approach it as a beginning blogger would be to treat it more like a blog journey. Chronicle all of the things that are working for you and not working for you. Let people follow you along from day 1.

The catch is, is it better to do this with the how to make money blog or a secondary blog? My gut tells me you should do it with a secondary blog but that means a bit more time. However, it gives you a bit more authority for when you are ready to launch your book or course.

Health and Fitness

Health and fitness is one of those tricky niches because you can get a ton of traffic from it, but it can be difficult to monetize if you don't know what you are doing.

Starting off the best approach to go is with affiliate marketing. This works well because your audience is actively searching for solutions to a problem and a nice Amazon (or wherever) link to a product that helped you can do wonders. A lot of blogs in this niche are usually run by teams of people or fitness trainers.

Choosing a niche for your blog can help it stay focused and relevant to your readers. However, for professional bloggers, the decision could also influence your income. Going into one of the more popular and profitable niches could make it easier to earn a living.

Chapter Six
How To Build An Affiliate Marketing Blog Overview?

Starting an affiliate marketing blog is actually quite easy. You can start an affiliate marketing blog in just a couple of hours or less. If you set aside an hour or two and follow this step-by-step guide to starting an affiliate marketing blog from start to finish, you will have your very own website all set up and ready to make you some money.

The trick, of course, is sticking with it. Starting an affiliate marketing blog is easy, but creating content over a long period of time is where most people fall flat.

Sharing your experiences and thoughts is now easier than ever. You might think that a blog is just a way to tell people about your interests and maybe find new friends that have the same desire for writing as you. However, nowadays blogs are more than just a writing hobby. They have slowly but surely become a way to make money from home without being an expert in the business. You can promote products and services and monetize your writing with a little effort and a lot of passion.

As you may know, affiliate marketing is a way to benefit from promoting brands through your posts, placing links in your texts, and monetizing visitors or customers who are led to the brand you are promoting through your blog.

Does it sound challenging? This is much easier than you think. We've prepared an easy guide on how to create your blog and start earning money using just your writing skills and a little bit of marketing knowledge.

When starting your affiliate marketing blog, it's important to do things in the correct order. Listed below are the steps I recommend you take, and I recommend you do the steps in the exact order that I've laid out.

Step 1. Defining your target audience and the blog niche

Starting from the very beginning implies thinking through your blogging development direction. The first step is to pick a niche and the people you will address your writing to.

✓ Pick a niche.

Think of the things you really like or you know a lot about. It can be anything in the world. The main point of blogging is passion and desire to work on something that brings you joy because these two things are the motivating forces that help you improve. The more effort you put, the more money you can earn.Second, narrow your theme to a topic that will be interesting for you but will also have a lot of opportunities for affiliate programs to sign onto. This is the step where you need to conduct research and find how many competitors there are in the field that you have chosen and what affiliate campaigns are available. Pick a niche in which you have a good amount of perspective and not much competition in terms of other blogs at the same time.Quick tip: You can also give yourself an opportunity to expand your niche by picking several related topics. For example, makeup and hair products, travelling and hiking, vlogging and content creation, etc.

✓ Identify your target audience.

After you've chosen your niche, it's time to clarify who your target audience is. This is not an easy thing to do, but a little research will give you an idea about who your readers will be and what information will be useful and valuable for them.The easiest way to do this is to follow the brands you want to get as your affiliate clients on social media and see who their customers or clients are. You can do the same thing with your competitors.Choose an affiliate program. A quick search will give you an opportunity to identify what affiliate programs you can sign for. Contact brands that might be interested in your service through their cooperation managers.

Step 2. Choosing a blogging platform and the domain name

When it comes to starting your blog, it's important to pick a suitable blogging platform. There are several platforms you can choose from; the most popular are:

✓ WordPress

✓ Joomla

✓ Wix

WordPress is the biggest blogging platform and offers a lot of opportunities and quick setup. It is designed specifically for blogging purposes and has a lot of different features that come in handy while creating your blog from scratch. Some advantages of WordPress are:

✓ Customizable design

✓ Built-in tools to control your blog

✓ SEO-friendly permalinks and mobile-optimized themes

✓ Multiple widgets are available

Joomla is used for creating websites but also includes an extension for blogging purposes. It's easy to use and has excellent flexibility alongside with convenience and usability. Wix in its turn has drag and drop templates, user-friendly interface, and free hosting.

Make a choice according to your needs and convenience.

A domain name is something you need to carefully think through as it will be the first thing your readers will see. Make it memorable, short, and related to your topic. Use a name that is well-understood when someone pronounces it – this way it is more convenient for people to remember your site when hearing about it in conversation. It will also be useful for a voice search, which has been progressively becoming popular. Pick a few names and discuss it with your friends and family before deciding which one is the best.

After picking your domain name, you should register it. You will see which domains are available and which are already taken.

Step 3. Designing and structuring

The design of your blog has a much more significant influence on your reader than you probably think. It not only presents your theme but also helps you to stand out from the crowd. If it is done correctly, your blog design makes people stay on your site longer and has a pleasing influence on your audience's attitude towards your content.

Quick tip: Don't use very vibrant colours, complex fonts, or a coarse background. Pick the colour combinations that will not distract from your content. Choose fonts that are easy to read.

Structuring your blog is also essential to make it organized. Decide what categories you need or what widgets you want to add. Add images or video-clips you think will be useful for your audience.

Step 4. Search Engine Optimization

SEO is one of the most essential things you should learn in order to run a successful affiliate blog. It helps to get more traffic and boost your earnings from affiliate programs.

There are a few tools you can and should use for your optimization, such as:

✓ **SEMrush** – This software will help you to get insights into your competitors' strategies in display advertising, organic and paid search, and link building. Also, it provides data on website traffic, backlinks, keywords positions. There are several helpful in-built tools; for example, SEO Content Template gives you ideas to write well-crafted content, optimized for search engines.

✓ **Moz** – A tool that is created to check your ranking score – links authority and the importance of your site in relations to others. Moz rank for each website depends on the number of backlinks, their value, and the domain authority. Moz scores each website from 0 to 10. The higher the value of backlinks is, the higher the score a site gets. An average score for a website is 3.

✓ **Ahrefs** – A tool that helps you monitor and analyze your backlinks and their types. It has its own crawler and provides a complete report on all of your backlinks and referring domains. You can check out your competitors' backlinks too. That way, you'll get an idea of what websites you can get backlinks from.

✓ **Google Trends** – A tool that is used to check the level of interest for a prospective keyword and find which keywords are getting more popular. It works the best with Google Keyword Planner. Though they are much alike, there is an essential difference – GT shows the relative popularity, which is the number of particular queries divided by the total number of searches of the same geography and time range.

✓ **Google Keyword Planner** – A software which is designed to build keyword lists for pay-per-click campaigns. It helps to build ad groups and find new keywords that you can add to your ad campaigns.

Try all of these tools out and decide which ones are the most convenient for you to use.

Step 5. Blog content

Good content is key. Every marketer knows that. In order to earn more from affiliate programs, you need to provide valuable and interesting information. The more users read your posts, the more they will follow affiliate links.

Be honest with your audience. Including affiliate

links so that they look good in your text, is real mastery. Be truthful when you speak about products and services, and you will get your audience's trust. Honest reviews are the key to making your content more credible.

That's why it's essential to know a lot about the products you promote. If you have the opportunity, try them yourself.

Be careful while using links and keywords. Don't clutter your text with keywords as they make it clumsy and rough. You want to make your content unique and easy to understand, that's why writing skills are very important.

Get help if needed. Some bloggers post a lot and use the help of freelance writers for editing texts to make great content every day. You can find such help on platforms like EssayTigers, Freelancer, UpWork, etc.

When putting affiliate links, remember to follow these tips:

✓ Make words or phrases clickable. Add anchor text – the visible clickable text in a hyperlink – to affiliate links; they look much better than a link itself.

✓ Don't put too many links – it's better to add

one or two links for a piece of content.

✓ Make links more noticeable, using bold fonts.

✓ Make your links look more neat or professional using link shorteners like Google Shortener, Bitly, etc.

✓ Use sidebars to make links more noticeable. However, you should be attentive to keep them user-friendly and convenient. Too many sidebars distract from content and annoy users.

✓ Use visuals. Don't forget to add visuals to your content. They help make your posts easier to digest even for boring texts. Using images or videos polishes up your blog and gives it a more interesting look.

We believe that everyone can start making money from affiliate blogs right at home. Creating a blog is interesting and exciting; making it a profitable hobby is even better.

Nowadays there are a lot of tools that will help you start your affiliate marketing blog and run it yourself without struggling. Even if you have no knowledge of creating websites you can easily make yourself a blog page with customized design and necessary options. Use this guide to start to monetize your writing right now without too much effort.

Chapter Seven
How To Do Online Advertising

Online advertising is one of the most effective ways for businesses of all sizes to expand their reach, find new customers, and diversify their revenue streams.

With so many options available – from PPC and paid social to online display advertising and in-app ads – online advertising can be intimidating to newcomers, but it doesn't have to be. WordStream makes online advertising easy, and we've helped thousands of businesses grow by leveraging the power of paid search and paid social advertising.

Online Advertising: Paid Search

When you think of online advertising, the chances are pretty good that you're thinking of paid search advertising. Paid search – also known as pay-per-click advertising, or PPC – is one of the most common and effective types of online advertising.

Paid search allows you to bid on relevant terms and phrases that may cause text-based ads to be displayed to users when they enter specific search queries into Google or Bing. These terms and phrases are known as keywords, and they form the basis of PPC advertising. Advertisers bid on keywords as part of an ad auction. This ensures that all advertisers have a fair chance of their ads being displayed to users, rather than those with the biggest advertising budgets.

Keywords should be highly relevant to your business, organized and structured into logical ad groups separated by campaign type, and aligned with the correct match type in order to be displayed to the right visitors, at the right time, for the right campaign.

Online Advertising: Paid Social

While paid search may have transformed Internet advertising, paid social is transforming the web of tomorrow.

Social networking remains the most popular online pastime for adults all over the world, and advertisers have evolved their strategies to target consumers where they spend their time, namely on social networks such as Facebook and Twitter. Paid social advertising functions similarly to paid search, with the notable exception that advertisers, not users, take the initiative – advertisers must "search" for users, rather than the other way around.

One of the greatest strengths of paid social advertising is the granularity with which advertisers can target prospective customers, and this principle underpins many social advertising platforms and products. Advertisers can target users with hundreds of parameters, from demographic data (such as age, gender, income, level of education, and marital status) to browsing preferences and social behavior.

Advertisers can also target users based on the types of pages and profiles they follow, the things they buy, and the news they read. These custom audiences can be created from existing customer data (to create "lookalike" audiences of similar users) to email lists, which Facebook and Twitter can pair with their data about these users to reveal greater insights about their behavior.

The rise of so-called "identity marketing" has proven to be the latest – and arguably, the most profound – shift in digital marketing of the past decade, offering advertisers unbelievable opportunities to grow their business.

Know Your Audience

Just as paid search advertisers have to conduct in-depth keyword research before launching their campaigns, paid social advertisers have to know their ideal customers inside and out to ensure that they're targeting the right audience segments with the right messaging. This is where buyer personas come into play.

Creating detailed buyer personas for your ideal customers allows you to go beyond surface-level information about your most loyal customers and delve into targeting options that allow you to target your prospective customers with a high degree of granularity. This not only allows you to maximize the effectiveness of your advertising spend, but also offers more relevant, targeted ads to your audience – recent data shows that people actually appreciate online advertising more when it's highly targeted and relevant to their interests.

Online Advertising: Campaign Elements

There is much more to online advertising than simply placing an ad on the Internet and hoping for the best. The most effective advertising campaigns combine numerous interconnected elements, all of which perform unique functions to maximize the campaign's potential. Not every online advertising campaign will have all the elements, but the following components of a digital marketing initiative will be common to many campaigns.

1. Text and Visual Ads

Google AdWords and Bing Ads offer advertisers the choice of either text-based ads or more visual advertisements, such as banners. Text-based ads are often referred to simply as PPC ads, whereas banners and similar ad formats are commonly referred to as display ads. In addition, social media platforms such as Facebook offer highly visual advertising formats that include some ad copy, which can be thought of as a combination of both. There are dozens of advertising formats available to today's advertisers, allowing you to choose the format and advertising network that best suits the needs of your campaigns.

2. Landing Pages

Landing pages are specialized, optimized web pages that visitors are taken to upon clicking an ad. Landing pages can feature specific products featured in the advertisements themselves, or they may include prompts for users to provide the advertiser with more information, such as web forms. Landing pages can be used to convince prospects to complete an action, such as making a purchase, or function as another step in a longer "funnel," such as requesting additional information or downloading a piece of content for lead generation purposes.

3. Call Tracking

To many advertisers, phone calls are the most valuable source of leads. For this reason, advertisers can choose to track phone calls generated from online advertising campaigns. WordStream Advisor, our comprehensive PPC and paid social management platform, offers fully integrated call tracking functionality, allowing you to determine the precise ad and keyword that prompted a prospective customer to call your business.

4. Sponsored Content

Many advertisers choose to utilize sponsored content as an element of their online advertising campaigns. Sponsored content can take many forms, from advertorial-style editorial content featured on websites (commonly known as native advertising), to sponsored updates on social media platforms. Both Facebook and Twitter offer advertisers this feature, with both platforms boasting a wide range of sponsored update options, such as Facebook's Promoted Posts and Twitter's Sponsored Tweets.

5. Analytics

Advertisers do not simply publish ads to the web and hope for the best – they must know exactly how well their ads are performing, and from where their traffic is coming. This is why analytics is a crucial component of any online advertising strategy.

Analytics tools are also invaluable in determining how consumers discover and ultimately interact with your website, a process known as attribution modeling.

6. Email Marketing

Email marketing is one of the most common elements in an online advertising campaign. Some advertisers launch email-only campaigns to highlight time-specific offers or content downloads, whereas others use email to complement their other digital marketing channels. Email marketing can be highly effective, making it a popular choice for today's advertisers.

7. Remarketing

Consumers rarely discover a website and decide to make a purchase immediately. The customer journey can be lengthy and complex, and take place across multiple devices and websites over prolonged periods of time. For this reason, remarketing has become one of the most important tools in a digital marketer's toolbox. Remarketing allows you to track users who have visited your website – but failed to convert or take action – once they leave your site, and serve ads to them on other websites. This not only significantly increases brand awareness, but also provides numerous further opportunities for the user to revisit your website and convert at a later time. Remarketing can be enabled on search and display campaigns, as well as social advertising initiatives.

Types of Online Advertising

There are many different types of online advertising, but which one(s) should your business use?

1. Display Advertising

Display advertising is a type of online paid advertising, typically using images and text. The most popular forms of display ads are banners, landing pages (LP's) and popups. Display ads differ from other ads because they do not show up in search results.

Most commonly, display ads are found on websites and blogs to redirect user's attention to the company's product. Working together with remarketing, display ads can have great success. According to Digital Information World, "website visitors who are retargeted with display ads are 70% more likely to convert on your website."

2. Search Engine Marketing & Optimization (SEM) & (SEO)

SEM and SEO are two types of online advertising that promote content and increase visibility through searches.

SEM: Instead of paying for the actual ad, advertising pay each time users click on the ad to their website. Businesses benefit by gaining specific information about their market.

SEO: To gain a higher rank in search engine results, advertisers use various SEO tactics, such as linking, targeting keywords and meta descriptions and creating high level content that other sites will link to. While SEM is a paid strategy, SEO is organic, making it a sought out type of online advertising.

3. Social Media

There's no doubt that social media advertising just keeps growing and growing each year. Consider these numbers: There are 1.65 billion active mobile social accounts globally with 1 million new active mobile social users added every day. According to the Hootsuite social media advertising statistics, social media advertising budgets have doubled, worldwide, from $16 billion to $31 billion in the past 2 years alone.

The two types of social media online advertising are organic, an online word-of-mouth technique, and paid. Placing paid ads, promoted posts or sponsored stories are a popular way to reach more of the demographic of the company, without paying a bundle. As you can see from the chart below, Facebook and Twitter are the most popular social media platforms for companies to reach potential new customers with LinkedIn a popular avenue for B2B sales.

4. Native Advertising

Have you ever noticed those sponsored ads at the bottom of blog or FB posts? They can be "other recommended readings" or "other people liked" with suggested examples for users to click on. This is native advertising.

5. Pay Per Click (PPC)

Pay per click (PPC) ads explain their concept right in the name. These are ads that advertisers only pay for when a user clicks on them, which contributes to the strength of PPC as a tool. If the ad was seen by 100 people and only 1 person clicked the ad, the cost of the ad revolves solely around the 1 who clicked. PPC ads are usually text, with a small image if at all. Keep in mind that 64.6% of people click on Google ads when they are looking to buy an item online.

6. Remarketing

Remarketing (or retargeting) is a type of online advertising that does exactly what it says it does. This cookie-based technology literally followers the user around the internet, in order to remarket him/her again. Statistics show that only 2% of web traffic converts on the first visit, which means 98% of users leave without converting right away. These users are targeted once they leave the website by then seeing subtle hints (ads), reminding them about their previous interest.

7. Affiliate Marketing

Affiliate marketing is promoting a company's product while earning a commission for each sale that was made. It's essentially a 3-party advertising agreement between the advertiser, publisher and consumer. It's widely adopted with bloggers who have large numbers of followers and are looking to gain passive income.

8. Video Ads

Video ads are growing in popularity, especially with the younger generation of consumers. BI Intelligence reported that digital video will reach nearly $5 billion in ad revenue and with the highest average click-through rate, 1.84%, of any digital format (2016). And the stats don't lie. 55% of consumers view videos in their entirety while 43% want to see more video content from markets.

How to Create an Audience

It might seem easy to start a blog. Ideas flow in and you get to write about your passions and what you love. Then you have a lot of blog posts but the problem is growing the audience and getting traffic to your blog site. Increasing web traffic other than your family and close friends can be a difficult thing, however, there are some practical tips that can help your blog develop, grow and even evolve into one of the most visited websites on the Internet.

6 Ways to Build Your Blog Audience

1. Syndicate Your Content

Blog syndication is when you put a snippet or just a piece of content of your blog to other websites. The main goal is to increase web traffic especially if you have just started a blog. You have a choice on how to syndicate your blog, but if you are trying to promote something like a product, then you can syndicate the entire article to give thorough information to your reader. There are many ways on you can syndicate the contents of your blog, but the most popular ones are through social media. This includes putting some of your blog contents to LinkdIn and Medium and so much more. There are also other

2. Blog Design

Your blog layout is a huge factor when it comes to attracting and increasing your audience. Your layout should be easy to use and anyone can navigate smoothly. You can do a Peek test to see what users do on your site. Most audiences when they visit your blog want to know the blogger's name and information which is usually in the "About" page, so make sure this is visible. Additionally, the usual menubar should be organized and the comment section should be easy to use.

3. Write For Search Engines In Mind

When you have a blog and your goal is to sell and market your products, Search Engine Optimization (SEO) is very useful. Most bloggers ignore this because it can be tricky and sometimes even pricey. However, a great turnout for web traffic is shown when you invest in content marketing. An increase in search rankings will soon benefit like inquiries for advertising and even inquiries for your

Jacob Green

products. All you have to do is just brainstorm some keywords that should appear in your blog and look for people who can find clever ways to help you incorporate these keywords into your blog site. Using an easy website plugin like Yoast SEO can make this much easier to garner a lot of web traffic.

4. Use Forums

Aside from SEO, using forums can be a great way to increase traffic as you start a blog. All you have to do is search questions that are related to your business topic and you can help people by answering them and even linking back to your website in the answer. This strategy is like hitting two birds with one stone. You are simply addressing their questions/problems and you are increasing web traffic to your blog at the same time.

5. Commenting On Other Blogs

Unfortunately, many people use the comment section to write spam comments, which gives a negative impression to this suggestion when starting a blog. However, if you are able to give a genuine comment, it is a great way to invite other blog writers back to your website or blog. As long as you are not overdoing it and invading all the comments sections of the website, forums and other blog sites similar to the niche you have, you will gain more viewers and make new friends.

6. Guest Post

Crossovers and collaborations are very important for bloggers. You may think it would promote competition, but it is usually viewed as connecting and widening your network to people or bloggers who are in the same niche as you. You just have to find a relevant and credible website and try to reach out to them by suggesting a relevant blog topic. You can write for free in the beginning and see from there how you can start earning extra from it.

These strategies are great ways to increase web traffic to your blog site. You don't really need to spend a lot to promote your blog. All you need is to persevere and expand your network to fully enjoy the benefits of blogging.

Chapter Eight
Mistakes To Avoid

Affiliate marketing programs are known to pay a good amount of commissions on a regular basis which makes it a lucrative industry for passionate marketers or world wide web lovers.

As lucrative as this industry is, beginners find it hard to figure out the right formula to get them started and maintain the right path. Most of the mistakes are not detrimental in the beginning but in the long run, they affect the returns on our marketing efforts more than we can afford.

Here, we have covered some most common mistakes that new affiliate marketers tend to make.

1. Working On A Niche that Doesn't Drive You

Affiliate marketing is a tough space, with many competitors out there promoting the same product, it is difficult to stand out amongst all and capture a fair share of the market.

You would have to be on your 1000% to make it

huge out there and if the Niche you are working on doesn't drive your passion then it will reflect in your content and communication. If you are passionate about what you market it becomes easier to target the needs of the users you are approaching and every day becomes an adventure.

2. Wrong Product Selection

Your product selection is completely dependent upon your targeted audience.

The product should add significant value to their lives or solve a problem that makes thing easier at their end. The right product selection will improve your conversation rates significantly and it will directly impact how much you make out of your efforts.

So, choose wisely and earn well.

3. Never Recommend What You Don't Trust

It's very important that you recommend products that you have used and that gained your trust as a customer/consumer.

Your hands-onapproach will guide you in creating a genuine recommendation which will help your audience making the right decision.

Another major advantage of this approach is a relatively higher retention rate which improvises your overall revenue and creates a healthy presence in the market.

4. Ignoring Helpful Resources

You are not in affiliate marketing alone, there are many affiliate marketers out there who are making a great living out of this profession. Many of them are spreading their experience and knowledge with everyone out there.

You should definitely keep on learning and experts recommend at least 30 minutes every day dedicated to learning. You can mix these learning sessions by learning about your Niche market, learning about affiliate marketing or learning other valuable skills like SEO.

5. Not Trying Things Out

While preparing marketing campaigns like social media ads, google ads or email campaigns, we often have many ideas to deliver the same message.

We often stick with the first good idea that came to our mind ignoring the other good ideas that followed the first one. This hurts our chances of coming up with a magical campaign.

So don't refrain yourself from trying things out, running two sets of infographics from the same campaign, using 2 subject lines for same email set, this will provide you with the most important learning that is self-learning.

6. Not Doing SEO

Having strong online presence is without a doubt is undoubtedly a prerequisite to deriving great out from your affiliate marketing efforts.

Whether you are working on social media or outreaching your audience via email campaigns, having anchored yourself in the gigantic sea of SERP iv very important.

7. Focusing On Only One Source Of Income

Focusing on your niche is very important which will definitely restrict you to the limited number of products to choose from. But that should not restrict you with only one or two products being marketed.

One must work to create multiple numbers of income streams by marketing multiple products focusing on the targeted audience.

8. Depending On One Source Of Traffic

As an affiliate marketer, you understand the value of quality traffic. The higher quality traffic simply means having higher conversion rates giving you amazing returns on your hard work.

The irony here is that good quality audience is scattered all across the pool of world wide web. You should always keep an exploring and deploy new source of quality traffic for your products.

9. Not Creating An Email List

Email marketing is considered to be one of the most personal mediums of connecting with your audience, giving you a chance of creating a genuine relationship with them. An affiliate marketer should always start creating their email list as soon as they start their journey as an affiliate marketer.

One of the most common technique to start building your email list is by implementing email subscription opt-ins on your website.

10. Not Having a Blog or a Website

A website or blog acts as a spokesperson for your products which keeps on promoting them on your behalf. Your blog or websites act as a permanent residence address allowing your audience to visit them whenever they require more information about your products.

Recent researchers have shown that direct search users have higher conversation rate which means a repeating customer tend to have more trust in your products then a unique visitor.

Creating a successful affiliate marketing business requires passion, commitment, knowledge of products, updated knowledge about market trends, relationship building with clients, quality traffic, and helpful product recommendations.

Many times, affiliate marketers with great products fail to make their business profitable just because they deploy detrimental strategies and the information is above is a small step to help them avoid these mistakes.

In a world of noise where everyone is selling something, it is very important to indulge in the race of making money but to for earning money but to help consumers/customers to buy what they actually need.

How to rank your blog in search engines above the competition.

Your customers are like everyone else in the world--they rely on search engines to find information. You've undoubtedly thought about the possibility of being one of the top-ranked entries on Google's

SERPs (Search Engine Results Pages), whether you're pursued a formal SEO (Search Engine Optimization) strategy or not.

Some of your competitors have likely used SEO to gain the top spots in Google searches pertaining to your industry--but that doesn't mean they can't be taken away, even if they've been at it for longer than you have. As you're probably aware, SEO has many facets, and there are several different paths you can take to overtaking your competition:

1. **Drive a Harder Content Campaign. Content serves as fuel for your SEO campaign.**

Google evaluates the quality, nature, and relevance of your onsite content to categorize and establish the authority of your site, and your ongoing content work builds on that authority. More content means more pages for Google to index, but only high-quality, original, well-researched content is going to add to your site's authority. Drive a harder content campaign than your competitors by doing more research, finding more original topics, delving into greater detail, and publishing more often. Eventually, you'll earn more authority, more online real estate, and more inbound links, propelling you to a better organic search position.

2. Get Better Inbound Links.

Link building is a necessary strategy for SEO, but there are several different ways to build and earn links. One of the best is through guest posting, the act of publishing content on external blogs. The value of links built this way is roughly proportional to the authority of the domain you're linking from; if you can get a link on a .edu domain, .gov domain, or a nationally recognized publisher, you'll earn more authority and a higher boost in rankings. Get many of these high-authority links, and you'll blow past your competitors (unless they've already earned similar links).

3. Use Social Media to Attract More Links.

Though quality is far more important in link building than quantity, quantity can come into play. The more links you have from different domains, the better your site is going to look to Google. Building hundreds of links, all on different domains, takes time and strategy, so consider taking a shortcut by letting your social media followers do it for you. Post your best content on social media, and consider using influencers and personal brands to spread that content even further. When people see it, and see the value in it, they'll be more likely to link to it--and if it goes viral, those hundred links could come to you in just a few days.

4. Cater to a Different Demographic.

Instead of competing directly with your competitors, try taking a bit of an angle on their approach. If your business model will allow it, consider targeting a different demographic. For example, if your main competitor has a hard lock on keywords related to marketers of well-established businesses, consider targeting new entrepreneurs or less experienced marketers. You can do this in the topic and keyword selection portion of your strategy.

5. Target Alternative Niche Keywords.

Similarly, you can target alternative keywords in your industry, with different products, services, or other offers. For example, if your competitor seems to pop up frequently for "solar panels," you could target more niche keywords like "monocrystalline solar panels." Doing so may reduce the number of potential viewers and visitors to your site, but will result in higher-qualified and converting traffic, and could give you the competitive edge you need to succeed in the rankings.

6. Offer Material for Rich Answers.

Organic rankings aren't the only way to get more visibility in search engines. Google relies on microformatting on websites to draw in what it calls "rich answers"--concise, objective answers to common questions and queries drawn in from outside sources. Implementing this formatting on your site isn't hard, but many modern businesses have neglected to do it; implement it, and focus on answering as many common user queries as possible in concise ways. Eventually, your answers will start turning up for those queries, and you'll get the credit for posting them (above the fold of organic search results).

7. Go Local.

Local SEO operates on a separate algorithm from national SEO. If your competition is national, you could go local to reduce the intensity of the competition and narrow your focus. Currently, Google offers up the top three relevant results for a local query in its local 3-pack. To get there, you'll have to ensure the accuracy and consistency of your NAP information (name, address, and phone number) on your site and on as many third-party directory and review sites (like Yelp or TripAdvisor) as possible. From there, you'll need to earn more positive reviews and write local content to maximize your chances of getting a local rank.

Though any of these strategies can feasibly allow you to outrank your competitors on search engines, don't be fooled into thinking it's a simple, fast, or easy process. Depending on how competitive your industry is, how authoritative your competitors' sites are, and how much prep work you've done in months and years past, it could feasibly take months or years of effort before you get results. But in the SEO world, as long as you're directing your efforts toward improving user experiences, complying with Google's standards, and ensuring the technical performance and structure of your site, your efforts will eventually pay off.

Conclusion

Constantly exploring the possibilities of improving the business is something that comes naturally to everyone running an online business. The online environment is the world that continually changes and anyone who wants to stay in the game needs to follow the changes and adapt. This leads to discovering new opportunities, one of those being affiliate marketing.

The starting point is examining your online business and how affiliate marketing can become a part of that business. Depending on the business type, some will choose to be merchants, while others will be affiliates.

Affiliates have their own workflow when it comes to affiliate marketing becoming part of their online business. It all begins with choosing the perfect programs. Those are the programs you can benefit from as you drive the right people to the high-quality products they will be interested in. The integration continues with the following processes:

✓ Implementing affiliate links in your content

✓ Optimizing the content with affiliate links

✓ Content promotion

As you are discovering the potential of affiliate marketing and how this monetization tactic pays off, you will soon stumble upon new products and programs worth exploring and promoting to your target group. Through content performance analysis, you will also be able to see which promotion strategy works best for your content.

When used effectively, affiliate marketing can help you monetize your blog. This enables you to continue creating content you feel passionate about, while also getting paid for it. However, in order to be a success, you'll need to go about it the right way.